*The Prostitute Murders*

# The Prostitute Murders

## The People vs. Richard Cottingham

ROD LEITH

Lyle Stuart Inc. Secaucus, New Jersey

First Edition



Published by Lyle Stuart Inc.
Published simultaneously in Canada by
Musson Book Company,
A division of General Publishing Co. Limited
Don Mills, Ontario

Queries regarding rights and permissions should be
addressed to: Lyle Stuart, 120 Enterprise Avenue,
Secaucus, N.J. 07094

Manufactured in the United States of America.

Library of Congress Cataloging in Publication Data

Leith, Rod.
The prostitute murders.

1. Cottingham, Richard, 1946-
2. Trials (Murder)–New Jersey–Hackensack. I. Title
KF224.C68L44 1983 345.73′02523 83-4984
ISBN 0-8184-0345-4 347.3052523

To my wife, Lori

# Contents

# Foreword

Richard Cottingham didn't seem the type, or so said the people who knew him. A former high-school athlete, a husband and father, a good provider and model employee; it just didn't add up. "Something's wrong somewhere," an old high-school classmate said soon after Cottingham's arrest in May 1980.

Something certainly was wrong, but not with the case against Richard Cottingham. The details that spilled out of court hearings and grand jury indictments described a man who had led an extraordinary double life, holding down a skilled job as a computer operator and supporting a wife and three children while he prowled Manhattan's red-light districts at night, looking for women to abuse and abandon.

There is nothing quite like the notoriety that comes with major criminal charges. Overnight, Richard Cottingham, then thirty-three, a quiet, cleancut young professional who had grown up uneventfully in the northern New Jersey suburb of River Vale, was a very well-known fellow. By the time of his indictment in September 1980 on charges of murder, rape, and kidnapping, his name was a household word in New Jersey.

Reporters and spectators crowded the Hackensack courtroom where he went on trial in May 1981. A sheriff's officer frisked the spectators, probing inside jackets and handbags with a metal detector. A year earlier, no one had known who Richard Cottingham was; now there was a chance somebody would try to kill him.

I was one of those spectators, though I had nothing personal against Cottingham. On the contrary, I was there, in part, to ensure that the accused got a fair trial, to record for the public what went on in court. The interest of my newspaper *The Record* of Hackensack, was not entirely altruistic, to be sure. The Cottingham case had become big news; it sold newspapers.

Anyone who has not observed a criminal trial is apt to underestimate the difficulty of proving someone guilty—especially when the crimes are grisly, when some of the evidence is years old, when key witnesses are prostitutes, and when the defendant is a local boy with a nearly spotless record.

There are more obstacles than one imagines to proving something, anything, "beyond a reasonable doubt," the Constitution's justifiably exacting standard for conviction. Evidence is destroyed or misplaced over the years, witnesses die or take ill, tiny acts of omission by police officers lead to legal challenges that threaten crucial testimony. Jurors burn out, lose interest, or contract cabin fever, particularly when a trial lasts beyond a few weeks and includes complex, sometimes monotonous testimony.

The state prevailed in the Cottingham case. But it was a closer call than it seemed.

Richard Cottingham was a cop's worst nightmare. He was crazy, although it was never proved, and he was mean. He was clever enough to get away with most things. He was, in fact, more than clever. He was a "highly intellectual" individual, to quote a judge who sentenced him to nearly two hundred years in jail after his first trial, at which he was convicted of three kidnappings, one murder, and several assaults.

His bosses at Blue Cross-Blue Shield of Greater New York said he was one of their most productive and valuable employees, capable of doing the work of any two other workers.

Even the police who pursued him for three years had to admire his ingenuity. It was as if he were planning his legal defense in advance.

Almost always his victims were hookers, the women least likely to refuse his advances, to make complaints to the police, or to make credible witnesses later on. He cruised for victims around Times Square and in Manhattan's Lower East Side, luring them into his car with the wad of cash he always carried.

A price would be agreed upon. Sometimes Cottingham warned the woman that his sexual preferences ran toward the rough and kinky (the lawyerly mind at work again—he would later claim that at least one of his victims knew what she was getting into). Then, typically, came a stop at a bar, where Cottingham would surreptitiously spike his companion's drink with barbiturates.

Soon afterward, the woman, sinking into unconsciousness, would be bundled into a car and driven to New Jersey. Some of the victims had a lingering, hazy memory of crossing a bridge before blacking out. The victims would awaken the next morning alone, in a motel room, on a roadside, in a parking lot, or on a sewer grate—bruised, beaten, partly clothed, and too groggy to be sure just how they wound up there. Those were the fortunate ones, it turned out.

In a variation on this scenario, Cottingham, rather than drugging his victim, would take her to a motel in New Jersey (some objected to leaving Manhattan but were swayed by his promises of generous payments) where he would tie her up or clap handcuffs on her. Then typically he beat, raped, and sodomized his victim. For some, he reserved the ultimate pain-reliever—at least two, he killed.

Richard Cottingham was arrested trying to flee a motel in Hasbrouck Heights, New Jersey, whose employees had called the police after hearing a woman's screams coming from his room. The victim was found bound and badly beaten but alive. Her screams had saved her life. Cottingham told the shotgun-toting policeman who confronted him that he had been with a prostitute and had gotten scared. A search of the briefcase he was carrying uncovered sets of handcuffs, pills, studded leather collars, and a leather gag. In his pockets were rolls of adhesive tape and a switchblade knife.

They didn't know it then,* but the police had captured the man responsible for a string of unsolved kidnappings, rapes, and murders in New Jersey and New York going back to late 1977.

Investigators in the office of the Bergen County, New Jersey, prosecutor went through their evidence vault and hauled out old hospital charts, blood-test results, and sworn statements from the victims. Slowly, inexorably, they perceived a pattern. These women who had been discovered, bruised and beaten and groggy—they had more in common than they knew. What had been considered by some as a series of disparate, seemingly unrelated crimes became a comprehensible whole. Each incident bore Richard Cottingham's signature.

A defendant with less money, brains and arrogance would have settled for a plea bargain. But Richard Cottingham believed he could outwit a jury and out-talk a prosecutor the same way he had duped his victims. He insisted he was innocent and his family believed him. They would to the bitter end.

Anna Cottingham, a stout, taciturn woman with a strong resemblance to her son, put her Florida retirement home up for sale to pay for his defense. She hired Donald R. Conway, a polished, distinguished-looking, top-dollar trial lawyer who had represented some of New Jersey's most celebrated criminal defendants.

Conway's adversary was Dennis Calo, a slight, wiry, obsessively hard-working young assistant in the office of Bergen County Prosecutor Roger W. Breslin, Jr. In contrast to the garrulous Conway, Calo sought no friends among the reporters at the trial and permitted himself only an occasional smile as he felt the jury

*Author's note: *As of press time, Cottingham has not been tried in New York*.

yielding to the building evidence. Calo skipped meals and regularly declined the dinner invitations his father, a small, tidy Italian gentleman who was usually among the court-room spectators, would proffer at the end of a day of testimony. "I've gotta work," Calo would say.

At the first of Cottingham's trials in May 1981, Calo produced four young women, three of whom were prostitutes, who identified Cottingham as their abductor. Fingerprints, blood and semen tests, and rug fibers from Cottingham's car supported the chilling testimony of these women who Cottingham had, in Calo's words, "littered" in motel rooms, alleys, and parking lots around Bergen County.

Donald Conway, a superb cross-examiner, discovered and brought the jury's attention to the many inevitable, small contradictions between what the women said at the trial and what they had told the grand jury that indicted his client. Then there was the inescapable fact that three of the victims were prostitutes. Conway did not miss the opportunity to question their veracity or to suggest they knew what they were in for when they got into Cottingham's car.

There were other unforeseen pitfalls for the prosecution. The testimony of one of Cottingham's earliest victims—a young housewife from Elizabeth, New Jersey, who had been abducted from Manhattan, beaten, and dumped unconscious behind a garden apartment complex—was challenged by Conway on grounds that a sheriff's officer had barred him from watching the woman as she identified Cottingham in a lineup.

The defendant had been deprived of his legal right to representation at a crucial moment, Conway argued; his lawyer had been unable to prevent the police from coaching or otherwise influencing the woman. Who knew what had gone on? Conway asked that the woman not be permitted to identify Cottingham as her kidnapper before the jury. It was one of those legal technicalities that have set many other criminal defendants free.

Superior Court Judge Paul R. Huot agreed that the sheriff's officer, and others connected with the lineup incident, including

Calo, had been "rude bordering on arrogant" in ejecting the defendant's attorney from the lineup room. But there was no evidence to suggest the victim had been coached, the judge ruled. It was one of those infrequent times when Calo permitted himself to smile. He had nearly lost his star witness.

Later in the trial, the judge threw out a rape charge because the state had no medical records to back it up. The county medical examiner had failed to write on the woman's hospital chart that he had found signs of rape during a physical examination. Normally he would have come to court to tell the jury firsthand what he had seen. But the physician had recently suffered a massive heart attack and was unable to testify.

Otherwise, Calo and his investigators had fashioned an air-tight case. When the defense produced Blue Cross records indicating that Cottingham was at work when some of the crimes were committed, the prosecution unearthed an old co-worker who testified that Cottingham frequently disappeared from the office for hours at a time. A former girlfriend said Cottingham had been with her on several days when the insurance company's attendance logs indicated he was on the job. Another former co-worker told the jury that Cottingham had once drawn a diagram of a New Jersey motel to show how he had sneaked out without paying the hookers he had lured there.

But in the end, it was Richard Cottingham himself who cemented the state's case. He took the witness stand late in the trial, gave an implausibly intricate alibi for one of the abductions (he had been arrested fleeing the motel and so could not deny taking the woman there) and flatly denied all the other charges, claiming he was at work, at home, or with a girlfriend on the dates in question.

His arrogance seemed limitless. Alluding to a fascination he'd had since childhood, the defendant launched into a lecture on the language and nuances of prostitutes and the curious practices of sado-masochism. He was careful to distinguish between the doers and the watchers, counting himself among the latter.

But Calo's cross-examination was masterful. By now thoroughly self-assured, armed to the teeth with evidence, he deftly demolished Cottingham's ingenious evasions. As the crowning blow, he seized on the defendant's claims that he had carried rolls of white adhesive tape with him so he could change and more comfortably secure his son's diapers—not, as was charged, to gag and bind his victims. Calo noted that Cottingham was carrying the tape the morning he was arrested in the Hasbrouck Heights motel. "Did you happen to have any Pampers with you at that time, Mr. Cottingham?" the prosecutor asked mordantly. No wonder that Cottingham's lawyers thought they saw jurors smirking with contempt at their client.

Richard Cottingham was doubtless as clever as the lawmen who so doggedly pursued him. But even he could not wish away the facts or persuade a jury to disregard the young women who, pointing a wavering finger toward the defense table, identified him as "the guy that beat me, that hurt me, that messed up my life."

MARK DUVOISIN
*Philadelphia*
*January 1983*

# Prologue

The door was open wide, allowing the dark, acrid smoke to escape into the hallway. Inside, the sound of a television could be heard, but the red glow was brighter than the TV screen. Fireman Jim Rogers and his partners, called to the fourth floor fire by a frantic chambermaid at the Travel Inn Motor Lodge, thought somebody was in the room. There was a lot of heat, so Rogers got down on his hands and knees and crawled through the doorway. "I could see a body in the bed, somebody was in the bed nearest the door," Rogers said, recalling that the smoke made it nearly impossible to make out the sex of the person in the bed. "I reached up on the bed and grabbed the body," the fireman continued, having discovered by then that it was a woman. "I dragged her out in the hall, it was quite traumatic. I realized what we had."

Fireman Rogers, a fifteen-year veteran of the New York City Fire Department, says he has never quite gotten over the sight of it. He placed the young woman on the hallway floor and quickly moved to administer mouth-to-mouth resuscitation. "When I saw there was no head," Rogers recalled, still finding it difficult to describe the ghastly experience, "I thought it was a mannequin."

Once Rogers and the other firemen attached to Rescue 1 had extinguished the flames and cleared the air in Room 417 of the Travel Inn, they had found the bodies of two badly burned people. Both were young women whose heads and hands had been severed. Someone had then poured a flammable liquid on the beds, carefully sprinkling the substance between the victims' legs. The bodies were severely burned around the buttocks, leaving the rest of the torso, legs, and arms almost untouched by the flames. There was no trace of the heads or hands, not even a spot of blood on the floor or in the bathroom. In the bathtub, someone had placed two piles of clothing, with a pair of platform shoes on each stack. But there wasn't a sign of a clue. No knife, scalpel, or any other kind of sharp instrument that might have been used to perform this grisly kind of surgery. Rogers, who has been promoted and assigned to another fire station in Brooklyn, says the shock of what he saw inside a Manhattan hotel room that Sunday morning, December 2, 1979, nearly caused him to undergo trauma counseling. A New York City fire fighter can become pretty hardened to death, especially in cases where the job requires him to retrieve the remains of fire victims. "I've never come across something like that," he insisted. "I hope I never do again."

On the street that cold winter day, word of the bloody torso slayings sent an extra chill down the spines of a certain group of working women. It didn't take long for these streetwise ladies to figure out who those two women were and what they were doing at the hotel at 515 West 42nd Street. West 42nd Street is to prostitution as Wall Street is to stock trading. "When I heard about it," said Jennifer, a willowy blond hooker intimately familiar with the neighborhoods of Manhattan's west side, "I stopped going to hotels over there. I worked only until 11 o'clock at night and I never go back to the Travel Inn."

This was a crime that sent shivers through all women such as Jennifer. Was this a lunatic who might strike again without warning? Was it some religious fanatic who felt it his duty to eliminate prostitutes in some grand scheme to put a stop to the oldest profession? He was both thorough and secretive, as if he had carefully planned the horrible deed. The great care he took to cover the crime intrigued the police. He removed their hands, leaving police with no fingerprints to identify his victims. He carefully, almost surgically, severed the heads. With no heads, there were no teeth to check with and compare to dental records.

Then he went one step further. He poured lighter fluid, or some other kind of flammable liquid, over the mattresses on the two beds in Room 417. The victims were certainly dead by this time. Did he strike the match as his final blow to their dignity? Or, as some investigators speculated, was this just the last step in a painstaking effort to assure that these two young women would never be identified.

The prostitutes and the New York police were not the only ones to wonder what kind of beast would perform such savagery. Dr. James A. Brussel, a Manhattan psychiatrist whose reputation in forensic psychiatry has brought him in contact with such nationally known criminals as the Boston Strangler, could hardly contain his curiosity about the mental makeup of the mystery man at the Travel Inn Motor Lodge. Who was this man who used a fictitious name and address when he signed in as a guest and kept himself so scarce that few people saw him during his three-day visit? "Why is he choosing prostitutes and why so savage?" Dr. Brussel asked himself during a conversation with a visitor. "He wants to clean up the sordid sexual mess of society," the psychiatrist suggested.

The person responsible for the torso murders became the number one target of a massive dragnet conducted by the New York Police Department. No stone would be left unturned. A task force of detectives was put on the city's biggest manhunt. So determined were the police in their search for the murderer that the task force included deep sea divers, assigned to plunge into the chilly waters of the Hudson River and other waterways around Manhattan and the metropolitan area in the seemingly fruitless hunt for the heads and hands of the victims. "We are going to keep knocking on doors and talking to people until we find the answers," New York City Deputy Police Chief Richard Nicastro told a reporter for *The New York Times,* adding, "We won't give up."

## *One*

# The Frustrated but Stubborn Cop

Women like Roberta and Diana seemed to make a habit of disappointing Paul Beakmon.* The detective had sat in courtrooms like this many more times than he cared to recall. He watched the lawyers as they shuffled back and forth from the hallway to the clerk's desk. He'd seen many of them before in the thirteen years he'd worked the precincts of Manhattan. Beakmon, a stocky man with a full head of hair that curled naturally when wet, had long become used to the drabness and the smell of courts. Nothing about them really surprised him anymore. He sat back and tried to relax while the bailiff dully read through the litany of names of

*Detective "Paul Beakmon" is a composite figure developed by the author to disguise the identities of several New York City policemen who assisted with information for this book. Any similarity between Beakmon and real police officers of the New York City Police Department is pure coincidence. All other police officers and others connected with the Cottingham cases are named in this book.

those with business before the criminal court this bleak morning in May, 1974.

But as defendants in other cases appeared to go through the motions of pleas for arraignment, Detective Beakmon discovered he was becoming uneasy. It was that same untraceable feeling he got in the pit of his stomach when he discovered he was wrong about something, usually something important. He waited. And the longer he sat there the more he tried to search his mind for what was causing his uneasiness.

He thought about the last time something like this had happened. Beakmon had considered the incident as a freak happening. Prostitutes were frequently roughed up by their pimps. And, on occasion, there were cases when a hooker would be hassled by a customer. The last one to come to Beakmon's attention was a young kid named Diana. She was barely seventeen and just fresh from the south. Like thousands of others like her, Diana had come into New York, lost, hungry, and ready for someone to reach out to catch her from falling. He always thought it was amazing how these kids got up the nerve to run from one problem right into the face of another. Diana was quickly coaxed into a stable. She was given a warm place to sleep and just enough money to nurture her junk food diet and her craving for new clothes. The rest of the money she demanded for her favors went to the man, her protector. Or so she thought.

Diana had been found beaten, bitten, sodomized, and robbed. She suffered a lot more grief and pain than she would have from a routine hassle. On the books, the incident was listed as an assault and robbery, but for the detectives of the morals squad and to the overlords of the world's oldest profession, it was more like an attack. It was an assault that shook the normally peaceful transaction of this illicit commerce, managed on the streets by cops and pimps, but controlled by the mob. A lot went by as routine in this jungle of panhandlers, dope racketeers, muggers, and con artists. But this attack could not. For as much as City Hall and a few judges might try, this trade wasn't going into bankruptcy. And as long as it thrived, the police had the obligation to protect its crucial source of productivity, the women of the streets.

The beating Diana took was far from the ordinary, and unusual enough for the vice squad commander to assign Paul Beakmon to find out why it happened. The detective had an easy time finding Diana, and even some helpful willingness from her pimp. The key suspect was a customer, or a john, as these men of all walks of life are universally and anonymously known. Diana said he came on very polite, almost innocently. She set the price, but he wanted more, much more than she was willing to have her body endure. A hulking man next to her fragile five-foot-three-inch, 106-pound body, he didn't give Diana much choice. Hardened by her few months on the streets, the prostitute nevertheless trembled as she described the man and his brutal force.

Beakmon hated this part of the job. Even though he had questioned prostitutes, to the point of harassment on some nights, he still accepted them as human beings. He had long given up trying persuasion and intimidation to get them to quit. He couldn't subscribe to the general attitude that nobody should care what hapened to a prostitute, particularly when he had to listen to this one's graphic details of torture from what seemed like an animal in man's clothing. The john was some kind of sadist, Beakmon concluded. But this guy did have one trait that puzzled the policeman. He listened as Diana described some cheap jewelry her attacker forced her to hand over after the assault was complete. It was some of that nickel-and-dime stuff you could buy at a counter in a cheap department store jewelry shop. Why, Beakmon asked himself, would some guy who had just paid fifty bucks for sex turn around and steal fifteen dollars' worth of colored glass?

Detective Beakmon spent the next several days canvassing the streets and the little coffee shops and dive hotels. Along the way he got a description of a guy from New Jersey who spent enough time and money around these streets for the women to remember his routine and car. He got Diana to look at some photographs. If Beakmon's hunch was right, this guy might show up in the records of some kind of street-related charge. That could mean thousands of mug shots, but at least he could narrow it down to a guy from New Jersey. His suspect would be about five-ten or five-eleven, muscular, and with reddish or sandy hair, depending on the light.

Diana was helpful when she looked over the pictures in the police mug books of possible suspects. She was nervous, but at least she showed up a few days later, when her alleged attacker stood behind a glass enclosure in a lineup with five other men. It was him, she blurted out with the degree of honesty policeman are accustomed to hearing from women who were violated so badly they still felt the pain.

Diana was such a helpful victim that Beakmon did something his seasoned police sense should have caught and corrected. He trusted a prostitute to show up in court. A month later, his stomach tied up in a knot, he knew he wouldn't make the mistake again. With an overloaded criminal court docket and more cases than twenty detectives could handle, Beakmon was beat. No witness, no hearing, and the case was thrown out; the guy from New Jersey walked his way out of Manhattan criminal court.

Beakmon thought immediately of Diana when it happened to another prostitute, six months later. This time, Roberta, an almost pudgy, nineteen-year-old blonde, was taken to one of those fast-trade motels on the west side. She was sexually assaulted, but not enough to prove in court. But she was found by a motel employee who was willing to testify that Roberta was in handcuffs, handcuffs that were used to imprison her while she was assaulted. A cop unlike Beakmon might try to go all the way on an assault charge booking, but Roberta didn't have the traces of bite marks like Diana. Beakmon went by the book. It was a case of unlawful imprisonment, according to New York State statutes. "Bondage," according to the rules played by those of the chic who are into sexual fads. And, curiously, as Beakmon found out when he went through the incident report by the uniform division, the woman had been robbed. Cheap jewelry again.

The handcuffs may have registered the first, troublesome clue that this incident was not routine. But for Beakmon the oddity in this case was the jewelry. He had never gotten to the bottom of that with Diana's beating. But he'd done enough leg work to save some time on this one. And although he'd felt more anger than disappointment with Diana, he decided to recruit her again. He'd enlist that strange code of loyalty the hookers seemed to respect. If he could get Diana to accept his theory that this guy was the one who beat her and that he was still at work—that if the victims didn't come forward and go to court against the accused, there would be more victims—maybe he could get Roberta's attacker and close Diana's case out too. If he could persuade Diana to talk to Roberta, maybe both of them would be willing to come to court.

Beakmon brushed back a few curls of hair as he watched the rain beat against the grey tint of the window panes that protected the inside of criminal court against New York's filthy air. It seemed an impossible task for those tiny droplets of water, thousands of them, as they banded together to cleanse the dirt-encrusted windows. It was a lot like his job, Beakmon mused, as he sat there in the courtroom absently fingering his stubborn curls. Out there was a city of millions, with just a few thousand to enforce the law. Each time a new raindrop hit the window, the glass seemed to grow darker with filth. The forty-three-year-old detective was suddenly frozen in a fit of hopelessness.

"The people versus Richard Cottingham," the bailiff mumbled, startling Beakmon out of his trance-like state. He rose from his seat and moved up to join the assistant district attorney, a balding man who, Beakmon thought, always seemed needlessly in a hurry when he was in court. The judge adjusted his glasses and shuffled some papers impatiently as the prosecutor leaned over to Beakmon and whispered, "Well, I don't think he's gonna be as patient with us this time." The judge had agreed to postpone the case twice in the space of three weeks. Both times the delay was caused, as far as the court was concerned, by the state's failure to produce the victim, its key witness.

Beakmon's idea to get Diana to hold Roberta's hand and assure the prosecution of its only chance to get a conviction made good sense. But Beakmon wasn't dealing with a couple of delicatessen owners who had both seen their stores robbed. That same sense of anger a couple of shop owners might feel about crime wasn't going to work with these two prostitutes. Beakmon suddenly found the reason for his uneasiness. He had done the leg work and found a suspect, but he had failed somehow in getting these women to recognize the importance of their civic responsibility. But was that his job too?

Until his alleged involvement in these incidents investigated by Detective Paul Beakmon, Richard Cottingham had a nearly spotless record in New York. One could almost overlook what happened back in 1969. Cottingham, then only twenty-two, was hauled into jail in Manhattan, so blind drunk he nearly cleared a sidewalk of pedestrians with his car.

But that was more than a decade ago. Now, Detective Sergeant Beakmon was working on one of the most gruesome assignments in the archives of New York City police investigations. Someone had killed two young women in a west side motel, cut their heads and hands off, and then tried to burn their bodies. Beakmon, working with a squad of detectives, was sent out to search mountains of garbage and miles of abandoned piers. No one could even imagine where someone who would commit such a beastly act would hide the heads and hands.

Beakmon would really have rather forgotten the assignment. Christmas 1979 was approaching and he was hoping that his daughter, Karen, who was nearly twenty now, would give up her foolishness and come home for the holidays. His daughter, unlike him in most ways, apart from her stubborness, was all he had left from a marriage that had ended ten years before. His daughter had taken off for the west coast, and ended up in San Francisco. Beakmon found himself more worried about her now than when she was living in a Greenwich Village loft apartment with some member of a rock band. At least when she was living in the Village, he could rely on his friends in the Manhattan South Precinct to keep an eye out for her. He thought often of her last letter, saying she had found a job with a sightseeing tour bureau.

But Beakmon hoped Karen would save up enough money, and homesickness, to come back east for the holidays.

For a solid week, since the two bodies were found by firemen on December 2, police scoured the city. Not knowing the names of the victims was bad enough, but what made the job tougher was the suspicion that they were prostitutes. If they were streetwalkers, chances are they would have had few friends—real friends, that is. The two women, both believed to be younger than twenty, could have been part of the daily busloads of kids who disembark at the Port Authority terminal on the west side. Kids came to the terminal from all over the country, rarely having anyplace to go and almost never knowing anyone in the city.

While one search went on to trace the identities of the victims, another hunt was on for the torso killer. The man left little behind. Room 417, on the top floor of the Travel Inn Motor Hotel on Tenth Avenue, was cleaned of almost all evidence. No finger prints, no weapons, and very few clues. All he left, really, was an address in New Jersey that turned out to be fictitious, and a name, Carl Wilson, that was probably just as bogus. Still there was one thing non-fictitious about the address. Could their suspect be from New Jersey?

Deputy Chief Richard Nicastro, commander of detectives for the Manhattan precincts, had the same task force of detectives that combed the piers for the grisly body parts go out to the streets and vice hotels. If the women were streetwalkers, there was the possibility some of their hooker associates might recognize the clothing the victims were wearing when found. Hookers were also questioned about being approached by a customer who wanted his sex at the same hotel. In addition, the women were asked if they knew of two prostitutes who disappeared suddenly. And because the victims were almost certainly prostitutes, Nicastro had some of his detectives review all the records for the last ten years of men accused or convicted of asssaulting prostitutes.

Carl Wilson, or at least the stranger who had used that name, had checked into the Travel Inn Motor Hotel on a Wednesday evening, November 29. Fortunately for the investigators, a few members of the hotel staff, accustomed as they were to the constant flow of customers who used the rooms of the blue and beige brick building for sleep and pleasure, took some note of this guest. He seemed to go out of his way to avoid conversation. He was rarely seen in the almost four days he rented room 417. The chambermaids hardly got a chance to see the room. The "Do Not Disturb" sign was left hanging on the outside doorknob most of the time. Employees were unable to provide any descriptions of any women seen with the stranger. But interviews with the staff and a few others who work in stores and taverns in the neighborhood of 515 West 42nd Street, the address of the Travel Inn, did provide a police composite drawing of the man who called himself Carl Wilson from Merlin, New Jersey.

The sketch was of a white male, about thirty-five years old, five-feet-ten-inches tall, weighing 175 pounds. He was described as having brown hair, which he kept neatly cut, with sideburns no lower than his earlobes. The description was of a man with a strong olive-colored face, with high cheekbones. The stranger was believed to be physically strong. Either that, or it was *two* men who somehow lured the two young women to the hotel, got them inside Room 417 and managed to behead them and cut their hands off. The stranger, if he worked alone, would either have to have drugged his victims or somehow knocked them out with forceful blows from his fists or some instrument. The amputations may have been done, police theorized, for two reasons: the murderer may have feared that identification of the women would incriminate him; or the ghastly deed, done with some surgical care, could be the work of a psychopath.

The police had their theories too about the victims and the killer's purpose in being at the Travel Inn. The victims, one of whom was finally and painstakingly identified as a twenty-two-year-old prostitute from Trenton, New Jersey, were either at the hotel with a pimp, or they were meeting there with a customer. The hotel is just a few blocks from the Port Authority Bus Terminal, a monument to travel in New York, where one can kill the time before catching a bus. There are several bars in which to have a drink, or one can pass time bowling, or shop in the many small boutiques and stores. The bus terminal is also a major job-recruiting station for the hundreds of pimps who help run New York's prostitution trade. A pimp could have picked these two young women out of the gangs of female runaways who arrive daily in the city and have taken them to the hotel for a sales pitch, maybe some drugs to coax them, maybe a little force if they proved too stubborn. But as the weeks of investigation dragged into a month, the majority of the dozen detectives assigned to the task force under Deputy Chief Nicastro had discarded the pimp theory. "We think a john did it, not a pimp," Cheif Nicastro told reporters more than a month after the bodies were discovered.

New Yorkers almost always have an opinion about a crime, particularly one that was touted as the most grisly in recent memory. But those of the city with the strongest opinion about the decapitation murders were the streetwalkers. The biggest understatement of the time came from the head of New York's police public morals squad, Captain John J. Ridge.

"He said we was *frightened?*" one black prostitute scoffed when she heard it. "Well, I'll tell you something, honey. I was scared as hell. I thought he was goin' home and makin' himself a Frankenstein whore." She was one of the many streetwalkers who firmly believed the stranger who checked into Room 417 was a homicidal maniac. And, while it didn't keep them off the streets, most prostitutes were far more cautious. Some who admitted to meeting customers at the Travel Inn said they refused to return there. Others said they worked in teams, sometimes losing valued time on the street while accompanying a partner to a parked car or to one of the many seamy flop houses and hotels that serve as instant brothels. And still others left New York altogether. One who said she came into contact with the stranger more than a year before the Travel Inn murders took off for San Juan, Puerto Rico.

*Two*

# A Good Cop Keeps Chasing a Hunch

In the rush of traffic that flows over the magnificent George Washington Bridge from suburban New Jersey to New York City each business day, one would hardly notice the man in the 1972 white Chevy Impala. Richard Cottingham, after all, was just another family man who paid his tolls, completed his tax forms, and worked to feed and house his family. He'd worked diligently at the same job for thirteen years with New York Blue Cross and Blue Shield. His field with the medical and hospital insurance firm was computers. While the job may have been a disappointment to William Cottingham, Richard's father, who was an executive with Metropolitan Life Insurance Company, the younger Cottingham found it rewarding.

During his thirteen years of service in the 200-member computer staff, Richard had acquired the reputation as an expert. His salary, while not outstanding, had risen gradually until he was earning about $25,000 a year. As a partial reward, his supervisors allowed him to report to the office at the hour of his choosing. Cottingham chose to work from 4 p.m. until 11 o'clock at night.

But unlike his fellow commuters, including those who rode buses and trains, Richard Cottingham didn't always make the return trip home after work. He knew the streets of the giant city like a cop. He commuted to Manhattan a good 240 days out of the year to his job, but he often went back on weekends and holidays. He began this as a weekly ritual about six years after his marriage to Janet, the mother of his three children. The pattern started just about a year after Jenny, Richard and Janet's only daughter, was born October 13, 1976. Once Jenny came along, Richard decided, much to his wife's dismay and frustration, that he no longer desired her as a sexual partner. Janet was never any striking beauty, and three pregnancies hadn't improved her chunky five-foot-two-inch figure, but her body was certainly not repulsive. Her husband, however, held to his decision. For nearly three years, the couple did not engage in sexual lovemaking. And if she asked or hinted at the subject, Cottingham would break into an outburst charging that his wife of a six-year-old marriage was totally undesirable.

Janet turned more and more to her friends and family for support. Both Blair, the couple's older son, and Scott were some help. Blair, born October 15, 1973, was in school by the time the Cottinghams moved to a three-bedroom house in Lodi, New Jersey. Janet Cottingham had been brought up in Queens Village in New York, and her high school friends she kept in contact with would occasionally visit the couple's home, nestled in a residential neighborhood near the Saddle River. But even these visits became painful. Her husband isolated himself in a room he had claimed for his own, and if he appeared during Janet's happier moments with friends and family, would either mock or ignore the conversation. He'd retreat back to his room, sometimes locking the door behind him.

It was after many of these confrontations with the usual result of his barricading himself behind the closed door that Janet started to become curious. She apparently made no mention of her discovery to the Hackensack attorney she eventually hired to handle her divorce. But Janet would later weep and sob about the time she dared walk into her husband's room to find an assortment of women's personal effects and clothing. The articles were never new looking and they were not gift wrapped. If they were not meant as gifts to her husband's mother, Anna, or his sisters, Kathie and Carol, to whom did these skirts, jackets, earrings, and necklaces belong? The answer to this question would not only solve the mind-wracking mystery for his wife, it would also ultimately link her husband to a series of sadistic crimes he had been committing since their marriage became for her an agony of lonely nights and fearful days.

Deedeh Goodarzi, a Kuwait-born woman of lovely dark features and an attractive five-feet-six-inch figure, had been selling her body up and down the east coast since she was a teenager not long out of Long Island's Mineola High School. One of her favorite working places was a massage parlor in Atlantic City, but her pimp in New York would usually find her after a few days of this luxury and drag her back to work the more lucrative streets of Times Square or the West Side. She was in Atlantic City during the last week of November, 1979, but decided this time she'd go back to New York on her own. She first took a train to Trenton, where her baby had been born the previous August. She visited for a day or two with a friend who had agreed to care for the child. Deedeh next boarded another train for the ninety-minute trip to Pennsylvania Station in Manhattan. It was November 30 and she reasoned that her pimp would be waiting impatiently. What she did not suspect was the fate that awaited her with the stranger in Room 417 at the Travel Inn Motor Hotel.

Deedeh had been raised by her maternal grandparents in Kuwait. Her guardians, who were Muslims, waited until their granddaughter was fourteen before allowing the youngster to join her father in America. She stayed only briefly in Mineola, Long

Island, where high school was made unusually difficult by strange customs and a new and awkward language. Before she was twenty, Deedeh, who was known as Jackie to her friends and Sabina or Jacquelyn to clients, had managed to be charged with prostitution and minor theft in geographic locations as far apart as upstate New York and California.

Whether the younger prostitute, the stranger's second victim, was already inside Room 417 by the time Deedeh agreed to accompany him to the Travel Inn is a detail that only the most careful pathologist could ascertain. Deedeh "Jackie" Goodarzi can't say and the stranger who signed himself as a guest the previous day won't reveal how the two women ended up side-by-side in the hotel room. It had taken law enforcement officials and detectives six weeks to discover the true identity of one of the prostitutes. The answers to other less pressing questions would have to be answered later. What was known is that Deedeh and her unknown colleague had met with a most brutal and savagely bloody end. One ranking New York detective remarked in gravely professional terms that the methods used in the double decapitation murder were unlike any mutilation murder in the New York metropolitan area in modern times.

It was about the time that a pair of hard-working missing persons investigators from Bergen County, New Jersey, had found the identity of Deedeh Goodarzi hiding away in a file of X-rays at a Trenton, New Jersey, hospital that Paul Beakmon began having his nightmares. The forty-nine-year-old detective had had a tough month. His daughter, Karen, hadn't come home for Christmas. Apart from the card she sent just before the holidays, he hadn't heard from her since Thanksgiving. He had been working day and night on the mutilation murder case and something inside him seemed to be coming apart. Sometimes it got so bad that he'd see his daughter's face on one of those helpless female corpses found mutilated and slightly charred on twin beds in Room 417.

But something more troubling was behind these morbid dreams of his. Detective Beakmon kept going over that fictitious address given by the man called Carl Wilson. "Anderson Place, Merlin, New Jersey." It reminded him of that scene in the movie *Taxi Driver*, the one in which Robert DeNiro has the comical exchange with the Secret Service agent in the Air Force sunglasses. DeNiro, seemingly wanting to impress, ticks off an address in New Jersey where information about joining the Secret Service can be mailed. The agent doesn't miss a stroke of the pen until DeNiro mistakenly or intentionally provides the agent with an eight-digit zip code number. What a queer coincidence, Beakmon thought. But what if Carl Wilson did it backwards, had given the false information, the fictitious Anderson Place in a non-existent town called Merlin, first, and the right state of residence, New Jersey? It wouldn't be far fetched. After all, Deedeh Goodarzi had lived in New Jersey and she had purchased her black, Phillipe Marco sandals at a Bamberger's Department Store in Paramus, New Jersey. It wasn't improbable that her killer could be from the same state.

Detective Beakmon had thought of those cases he investigated in 1973 and 1974. Roberta and Diana were names that conjured one of the most disappointing experiences of his police career. Thinking about those episodes wasn't easy, even though his colleagues, and even his boss at the time, couldn't blame him for failing to get a conviction. The two cases—robbery, sodomy, and sex abuse on September 4, 1974, and unlawful imprisonment and robbery on February 12, 1974—were among the hundreds of old charges reviewed after the Travel Inn mutilation murders. These two cases had been sealed by order of the Manhattan District Attorney's office, but secret or not, policemen, like veteran reporters, have their own methods of finding case jackets and files. Richard F. Cottingham, Beakmon recalled, looking at the file, worked in New York, lived in New Jersey. Beakmon could find no more charges filed against Cottingham in New York. He had a friend with a contact in Bergen County, New Jersey, check the state's Bureau of Criminal Identification. BCI showed nothing more than a shoplifting conviction against Beakmon's suspect. His date of birth was 11/25/46, he was married, with three kids, and was steadily employed by Blue Cross-Blue Shield in New York since 1966.

Paul Beakmon already knew the official response to this one. In police parlance, the guy is living across the river in Jersey. He's been clean, in New York, as far as rap sheets or arrest records are concerned, since 1974. Gainfully employed, he likely is considered a respected member of his community. In short, Beakmon knew he'd have to have a lot more than dusty old charges of sodomy and handcuffing prostitutes six or seven years ago in order to convince his superiors that he should bring Cottingham in for questioning.

Still Detective Beakmon couldn't forget that baby face and stocky build. He measured that visual impression against the composite sketch of the stranger who horrified the Travel Inn the weekend of December 1, 1979. He tried to persuade himself that the similarities were just a coincidence. But his old companion, that gnawing sensation that followed him when he had a hunch or caught himself in a dreadful mistake, kept after him. It stayed with him until four months later, when word of a major arrest in New Jersey got to the squad room at the Tenth Precinct station house.

The New Jersey break in the Times Square torso murders (as they came to be known, even though they took place blocks from Times Square) did not come before New York authorities were confronted with another mutilation murder. The victim, Jean Mary Ann Reyner, was a twenty-five-year-old prostitute who used the Hotel Seville on East 29th Street as one of her headquarters. She was stabbed to death on May 15, about five and a half months after the stranger struck at the Travel Inn. Jean Reyner had been mutilated, her breasts removed in what police sources described as the work of someone who took care to cut them off slowly, with near surgical skill. Sgt. Edward Dehlem, who would head a team of detectives on the Reyner investigation out of the 13th Precinct, made certain to have his men study the composite sketch of the man identified only as Carl Wilson.

And unknown to New York detectives was the investigation underway in New Jersey into the May 4 strangulation death of a young woman in a motel room in Hasbrouck Heights. The woman, later identified as Valorie Ann Street, but known to authorities initially as Shelly Dudley, had been picked up while soliciting on 32nd Street, near Madison Avenue in Manhattan. New Jersey authorities were perplexed over the nature of the crime and were unable to properly identify the body, which was found stuffed under the bed in a motel room. However, the crucial break for local police and detectives with the Bergen County homicide squad came on May 22, 1980.

*Three*

# Two More Motel Rooms, Two More Murders

It was about 9:20 into a Thursday morning, May 22, and Patrolman Stanley Melowic had just received what would become the most important call of his thirteen-year career. He put the accelerator pedal of his police cruiser to the floor, rushing ahead of traffic on Route 17 in Hasbrouck Heights. The trip to his assignment took just two minutes, but those precious seconds seemed like an eternity to Leslie Ann O'Dell. Leslie had just finished enduring almost three hours of savage torture in Room 117 of the Quality Inn Motel. Her body was trembling. The pains ran up her back to her neck. Her right breast was bleeding. She was living a nightmare that started in New York City with a man who was going to change her life.

Leslie Ann O'Dell, a blond, pale-skinned kid of eighteen, had come to New York from Washington State by way of Washington, D.C. She disembarked from a Greyhound bus at, where else

. . . the Port Authority terminal. Her arrival was near dawn on May 18 of 1980. There she just sat on a lonely bench and wondered what to do next. She had no money, and by now she was regretting the fight she had had with her boyfriend, when a tall, handsomely dressed black man named Jimmy approached the bench. Jimmy said he was twenty-one, but to Leslie he seemed older. He was kind and understanding. He offered to buy her breakfast and she gladly accepted. Before Leslie knew it, she and Jimmy were chatting like close friends. He invited her to come to his father's place in New Jersey. Leslie didn't know where the place was. She hardly knew where New Jersey was. That night, Leslie, in New York City less than twenty-four hours, had her opportunity to try a new career. As she put it, "I had to try out in the streets to make some money for him."

Leslie was shuffled around Manhattan for another day, passed on to another pimp named Kenny. Jimmy, the recruiter, went back to his "employment agency" at the bus terminal. It was on her fourth night of street-walking when Leslie met a man who called himself Tommy. He pulled up in a blue and silver Chevy Caprice as Leslie was soliciting at the corner of Lexington Avenue and 25th Street. He told her he didn't much care for the neighborhood they were in, an observation that Leslie found agreeable since the streets were frightening to her. Tommy suggested she join him in the car and that they find a bar to talk in.

It took a whiskey sour and a little time, but Leslie started to trust this guy. He had sandy hair and a neatly trimmed mustache. He talked about his house, a regular job, and a few girlfriends. Leslie translated this into two observations; he wasn't queer and he wasn't a pimp. She decided to like this guy and she was pleased when he suggested they head over to New Jersey because it was away from New York. If she wanted, he said, he would take her to a bus depot over there. She liked the idea, because Leslie was afraid she would meet up with Jimmy again if they went back to the New York bus terminal. "It was really nice that I'd found someone who would help me out of this mess I was in," Leslie would say later, relating her story. But then she repeated what her new-found friend had said in response, and she realized too late that she should have taken the remark as an omen. "Well," he told her, "you'll do anything when it comes to a life and death situation."

Leslie and her friend sat at the back table at the bar for a few more drinks before they walked back to his car, around three a.m., and headed off to the George Washington Bridge. Somewhere along the way they stopped at one of those highway restaurants for a bite to eat. He again consoled her, although it became clear to Leslie by now that he was also interested in sex. But Leslie figured she would need the money and was willing to oblige. The negotiations started at $50 for a half-hour, and reached up to $100. Leslie was hungry, too, and her craving was satisfied by the steak, french fries, and Coke she devoured while they sat, bartering over her price, in the diner off Route 17. It was getting light out when they arrived at the Quality Inn. The desk clerk later recalled that a man with sandy hair, dressed in a grey sports jacket and brown slacks paid the $27.77 bill for Room 117 with two $20 bills.

They entered the motel from the rear and went to the room, where Leslie freshened up and had a cigarette while he went back out. He said he wanted to move the car around to the front of the motel. When he returned, he was carrying a paper bag and an attaché case. In the bag was some whiskey, but Leslie would soon find out what the attache case contained. They both disrobed and she crawled into bed, tired from the tricks she had turned the night before and from the long morning. But she was still willing to earn $100. She thought it was very considerate when he told her to roll over on her tummy, he was going to rub her back.

Suddenly, she felt all of his 180 pounds pounce on her back. She felt a sharp instrument at the back of her neck and heard the sound of something jingling. Then there was a click as a pair of handcuffs were clamped around her wrists. Leslie tried to remain calm, telling him it didn't have to be this way. He didn't have to hurt her. But she quickly learned that it would have to be this way.

She later described a voice that sounded rough and low. "You have to take it," he told her, holding the knife to her throat. "The other girls did, you have to take it too. You're a whore and you have to be punished." Leslie felt the knife pressing to her throat as he ordered her not to scream. She fought back the desperate need to scream as he told her he was going to beat her very badly, cut her and leave scars on her face, her breasts, her vagina, and her anus. He was going to cut her uncountable times. Just too many times, he threatened.

Leslie's body quivered as she felt herself imprisoned by his weight. She promised not to make any trouble, but she might yell out from the pain, she told him. The metal cuffs were starting to cut into her wrists as he forcefully rolled her body over and brought his foot down on her neck. This was just one of the moments when Leslie thought it was all over. He brought the knife to her breast, pressing it firmly enough to leave its mark. She fought to hold back a scream as he squeezed and bit her breasts. She shuddered from pain as her right nipple spurted blood. Leslie tried to concentrate on something else. Closing her eyes, she thought about her fight with Bob. How silly their lover's quarrel seemed now. Her mind continued to drift as he rolled her back on her stomach again and pressed his body onto her frail, 118 pounds. Her legs were spread and she felt him enter her from the rear. It was the first normal sexual act from him since they undressed.

Leslie had made her mind up the night before that she would get away from the pimps and the career they offered. Like many young girls today, she had got to know about sex as she was entering high school. It never carried much meaning for her. A short, physical act, with little pleasure. But she never remembered its being painful. Even the first time wasn't painful, just disappointing. And those first few times with customers picked up off the streets were a total washout emotionally. Afterwards, it became a drudgery. Older men, as old as, or older than, her father, paying her for what? She just couldn't understand why. And then the money, except for a few bucks for food, had to be handed over to Jimmy or Kenny. And what did they do for the money? Leslie didn't care anymore. She just wanted to get away.

The motion suddenly stopped and he toppled off her, breathing somewhat heavily. He rested there, as if he had come in from playing tennis or jogging. In the silence, he slowly stroked his penis. She wondered what he was thinking and she thought of how she might get away. These thoughts racked her brain simultaneously. As Leslie lay there on the bed, deep in her desperate thoughts, she hadn't any idea of the horror that had happened previously in this very motel.

She knew she wanted to escape the world of prostitution Jimmy had introduced her to a few days before. She wanted to get away from that. This present torture was just the final reason. She couldn't possibly imagine that there could be a deadly common thread between this stranger next to her in bed and the sleazy life of the streetwalkers of New York City. She never dreamed that she might be the last in the bizarre succession of abductions, brutal assaults, rapes, sadistic sexual attacks, and bondage that had terrorized the ladies of the streets.

Yes, Leslie Ann O'Dell would be the last of a long list of victims, but the question was whether she would live to tell about it. Would Leslie, like nineteen-year-old Valorie Street, who was tortured and strangled a short three weeks before at the same motel, never leave the motel alive? Would she, like the three other prostitutes murdered in New York, become another silent victim?

She stared up at the ceiling as he lay beside her, a few inches away in the double bed of Room 117. He had been silently playing with his penis for what seemed like an eternity. But, like a thunderbolt, the silence was broken. His anger seemed more violent and threatening as he railed at her about being a prostitute who needed to be punished. He grabbed the thick leather belt from his pants and told Leslie what she needed was a good beating all over her body. She needed to feel pain, just like the others. The handcuffs and threats were not enough. Leslie whimpered and begged. It wasn't necessary, she again pleaded. She could feel his hot breath as he lay on top of her, forcing his penis into her anus. If only this was all, she thought, as he heaved and thrust his hulky body, sending shooting pain through her insides.

All of a sudden he fell silent as he sodomized her. He didn't say a word as he rose from the bed and walked to the bathroom. He came back, wiping his face with a wet washcloth. Beads of perspiration disappeared from his face and neck as he ran the cloth along his skin. He walked over to Leslie, her hands still imprisoned by the handcuffs, and gently wiped her face. It was soothing, she thought, but it was maddening, this instant flash of kindness from him. He stood there for a few moments, staring down at her face. She managed a slight smile of appreciation. The gesture was strained by the frightful suspense of what would be next.

He reached his powerful arms for her body and rolled her over, her face toward the wall. But she could see out of the side of her eye that he had reached for the attaché case by the bed. He fumbled inside the leather case and retrieved a black pistol and another set of handcuffs. He fastened the cuffs around her ankles, saying he would use the gun to blow her head off if she resisted. She pleaded again, but he just got more enraged, telling her to shut up. He was going to torture her some more. She had to let him do whatever he wanted to her. If she let one more word out, he would put a bullet through her head. He removed the cuffs from her wrists and lay down by her, pulling her body over next to his waist, ordering her to lick his penis. Leslie followed his order, caressing his penis with her tongue as he lay there watching. After some ten minutes of this, he commanded her to get down on her knees on the floor. He told her to lick his back from his neck down, and she again followed his directions without a whimper of protest.

She was just like the slave he wanted. He told her he was the master and she was to do anything that he wanted. He ordered her to lick his feet. He lay on his stomach on the bed, with Leslie on the floor, kneeling over his body. As she silently caressed his toes,

Leslie took a glance around the room for the first time. She tried to spot something heavy enough to hit him and knock him unconscious. She alternated lifting and holding his feet with one hand, then the other, as she felt around under the bed for his leather case. She got hold of it and felt around inside and found the pistol. It was light in her hand as she pulled it out and stuck it by her knees, out of sight.

He had tired of her licking him and ordered her to stand up and come over toward him. Leslie hesitated for a second, not knowing what torture he would think of next. She had never handled a weapon, much less shot at someone. But she was desperate. She didn't know what he wanted next. She pulled the pistol out as she rose and pointed it at him. He was startled, but he started to get up, ignoring her orders not to move from the bed. As he came toward her, Leslie squeezed her finger on the trigger with all her strength. She pulled again, but nothing happened. He grabbed his knife and came after her. "Oh, God, no! Oh, God!" Leslie screamed.

Eleanor Cykewick was the first to hear the screams. She was making her usual morning rounds of the rooms along the corridor near Room 117. It was about nine o'clock and most of the businessmen, the usual customers on a weekday, had checked out. Eleanor was coming out of a nearby room when she heard a woman scream. She walked toward 117 and heard muffled voices. Eleanor didn't dare open the door. The maid, who like the other women on the staff of the Quality Inn was still terrified over the recent murder in Room 132, did the next best thing. She called to the front desk.

He was in a rage now, no longer startled by Leslie's momentary bravery. He threw her on the bed and came down on top of her. She gagged as he pressed his hand to her mouth. "If anyone comes to the door," he snarled, "you're dead." Leslie trembled uncontrollably. There wasn't anymore she could say to him. It was past the point of her doing anything more to please him. What was there left? Begging just seemed to spur him to greater anger. Leslie had almost drifted into unconsciousness when the silence was interrupted by the telephone. "Tell them everything is okay," he blurted, handing her the phone.

Todd Radner, the motel's assistant manager, was on the telephone to Room 117, with Paula DeMatthews, the head housekeeper, standing nearby. Screams were heard coming from the room, he told Leslie, detecting a trembling in her voice. Radner wasn't persuaded by Leslie's strained response. He told Leslie that the motel security would be sent to the room. Radner and the head housekeeper headed quickly for the room.

He could only hear one side of the conversation, but when Leslie said, "That would be fine," the stranger went back into his rage. He slapped her across the room, sending her tumbling onto the bed. Just then, a knock came on the door. He told her to answer it, but to leave the chain attached. Mrs. DeMatthews and Radner stood outside, just barely getting a glimpse of Leslie's face, by now reddened around the eyes and puffed by the blows.

"Everything is okay," she lamely told them. "I can't open the door. I have no clothes on." Paula DeMatthews moved forward, and Todd Radner told Leslie he would stay outside, the housekeeper would come inside. "I can't open the door," Leslie insisted. "Well, we have to see you," Radner said, trying to stall for time. "We just have to know you're all right," he said. Both he and Paula DeMatthews watched the victim's gestures. Leslie was pointing her thumb back, trying to indicate with her finger for the two to go for help. She hoped they had gotten her message.

The stranger was in a panic. He held the knife to her back and told her to call the desk. She picked up the phone and got Todd Radner again. She seethed with pain as he pressed the knife into the small of her back. She repeated what she was told. "Everything's okay now. I just had a fight with my boyfriend." She dropped the phone and collapsed on the bed. "Are they coming," he demanded. Leslie lay there for a few second, trying to make every bit of precious time count. He asked again. "Yes, they're on their way," is all she could think to say.

Patrolman Melowic pulled his cruiser into the parking lot of the Quality Inn off Route 17 and was about to drive up by the office. But he saw a small gathering of people in the southeast corner of the building, near the rear of the motel. Todd Radner was one of them. The assistant motel manager was waving frantically to the policeman as Melowic drove over and started to get out of the car. Radner ran around to the driver's side and told the cop what was going on inside. The patrolman picked up the microphone to his two-way radio and called into headquarters for a back-up. Then he reached under the dashboard and retrieved a twelve-gauge shotgun, loaded it, and got out to rush with Radner to the back entrance of the motel.

The stranger scurried around the room, tripping as he got his clothes on and gathered up his attaché case. Leslie cowered on the bed as he threw the knife and some pieces of clothing into the case. She waited until he approached the door. Jean Bujkowski, another maid, was a short distance down the corridor as he opened the door and started into the hallway. He panicked when he saw the maid. "Get him! Get him!" Leslie screamed from the doorway. "Stop him! Stop him," she shouted. "He tried to kill me."

He didn't stop or even turn back toward Leslie. He raced on past the maid.

The Quality Inn Motel sits in the center of one of the nation's busiest suburban regions. Hasbrouck Heights, in New Jersey's Bergen County, is intersected by two major highways and a federal interstate roadway. It is home for warehouses and office buildings of some of the country's industrial giants. One of the country's most energetic business jetports is located in nearby Teterboro and the giants of industry are a short commute to Newark and New York. New Jersey's booming sports complex, The Meadowlands, is in nearby East Rutherford, and the football Giants stay at the Heights Sheraton, in Hasbrouck Heights, when they're playing at their stadium at the complex. Hasbrouck Heights, statistics will confirm, has its problems with pollution and traffic, industrial crime and small-time mobsters, but it doesn't host a murder very often. When it does, the event marshalls the full effort of its tiny police force and brings in support from the county's sheriff and prosecutor.

On May 5, eighteen days before Leslie Ann O'Dell found herself a prisoner in Room 117 of the Quality Inn, the police of this small borough and Bergen County authorities had more than they could deal with for a Sunday, any Sunday. That was the day they found the nude body of a nineteen-year-old woman stuffed tightly under a bed in Room 132 of the Quality Inn. They knew her only as Shelly Dudley of Florida, this limp and brutally beaten body of a white female. She was bruised over most of her torso, bleeding from one of her breasts. She was naked, handcuffed, and her mouth was sealed shut by white adhesive tape. She had checked into the motel between four and 4:30 in the morning, wearing jeans, tennis shoes, and a simple white blouse. That and the fact that laboratory tests would show she had had anal and vaginal intercourse not long before her death and that she had severe human bites on her breasts, so savage that they almost tore off the right nipple, were all the details the police had. Room 132 was cleaned out. Police could find no clues.

"The room was totally cleaned out, even the room key," a bewildered Roger W. Breslin, Jr., the chief prosecutor of Bergen County, announced at a press conference on May 5, 1980. Breslin, whose office had failed the year before to convict Dr. Anthony Jascalovich, in the famous "Dr. X Case," ordered his investigators to trace the identity of the victim and what brought her to the Quality Inn at four o'clock that Sunday morning. The prosecutor's people also sent the handcuffs off for examination to determine if the killer had left any latent prints on his torturous device. These were the only leads Breslin's people had.

The woman's clothes, belongings, and luggage, if she had any, were not found at the motel. She had given a street address in Florida when she signed the motel register as Shelly Dudley, but she gave no town or city. Florida authorities could be of no assistance, since the name the woman gave didn't show up on any police arrests and the street address could have been one of several dozen in Dade County alone. Investigators also made the rounds of a few dozen bars and taverns on the Route 17 strip, between Route 46 and Interstate 80, both of which are heavily travelled roadways into New York City. But no one reported seeing the woman or seeing anyone of her description getting a ride to the Quality Inn. Except for the desk clerk, who charged a woman called Shelly Dudley $25.20 for room 132, no one reported seeing the woman after she headed for her room.

The mysterious strangulation murder brought back unwanted memories for the police in Hasbrouck Heights and the investigators in Prosecutor Breslin's office in nearby Hackensack, the seat of sprawling Bergen County. A few years before, in the parking lot of the Quality Inn, in a brushy area near Route 17, a motel patron had stumbled on the body of young and beautiful nurse. The corpse of the twenty-six-year-old woman was a graphic example of what every cop with a wife or a young daughter feared. She was a helpless victim who was apparently overpowered, bound at the hands and feet, and suffocated until her lungs collapsed. Maryann Carr, a nurse for a prominent Englewood physician and the wife of only fifteen months to a young Little Ferry businessman, was discovered dead on December 16, 1977. Besides the shocking reality that murder could strike again in their ordinarily quiet and safe bedroom suburb, the police resented being reminded of the crime for one other burning reason. The Carr murder had never been solved.

The fact that they were totally stymied by the sadistic torture and murder of the nineteen-year-old-woman who called herself

Shelly Dudley did not prevent the police from rushing to find links between this crime and the murder of Maryann Carr: Both women had ended up at the Quality Inn. Both were either strangled or suffocated. The hands of both victims had been shackled with handcuffs. Now, with the scent of Shelly Dudley's brutal murder still fresh, detectives in Hasbrouck Heights and Hackensack were finding themselves encouraged that they might close the book on the unsolved 1977 murder if and when they found the beast who had ravaged this young woman's body and crammed it under the motel bed.

Stan Melowic was a cop who took precautions. He peered through the glass door at the rear entrance to the Quality Inn and found the corridor on the first level vacant. He double checked his shotgun and pushed the door open. The policeman slowly moved forward, pausing to catch each sound. His ear picked out the sound of keys jingling. The noise was coming closer. Someone was running towards him. Then the source of the jingling came into view. He was a large white male, probably 180 pounds, but more important than his bulk, the man was carrying what looked to Melowic like a small caliber pistol. The policeman retreated a dozen feet or so and raised the shotgun.

"Hold it right there and don't move," Patrolman Melowic shouted. The unidentified man took just a few steps forward, coming to halt a few yards away from the barrel of the chest-high shotgun. The man froze in position against the wall, a spread-eagle stance, as the policeman later recalled, making the observation that this man was not ordered, but automatically assumed the police arrest position. Melowic took the pistol and tossed it across the corridor. The stranger stood motionless and stone silent as Melowic laid down his shotgun at a safe distance, replacing it with his service revolver. He brought the man's hands behind his back and handcuffed them together. The cuffs broke the man's silence. "I didn't do anything," he blurted in protest. "I was with a hooker and got scared."

Leslie Ann O'Dell was in total hysteria by the time Sergeant Edward Chermark, Partolman Melowics's immediate superior, walked into Room 117. She was sitting on the bed with a sheet wrapped around her body. A maid was seated next to her trying to give her comfort. She sobbed and trembled as the sergeant entered the room, complaining to him that the handcuffs hurt her wrists. Chermark reached over and tried his own handcuff key, but it failed. He left the room for a few minutes, returning with a key he had taken from the stranger who was seated in the foyer a short walk away with Patrolman Melowic standing guard. He placed the key in the handcuffs and Leslie's hands were free again after nearly three hours of torture.

"He said he got off on hurting girls, seeing them in pain," Leslie told the police, breaking into an hysterical cry under the questioning. Before Leslie was taken to a nearby hospital, she identified the 1979 Chevy Caprice, silver with a blue top, that had brought her to New Jersey earlier that morning. At the hospital, in neighboring Saddle Brook, Leslie was treated for a bruise on the neck, a knife cut on the right breast, a puncture in her lower back, and a savage bite to her right nipple.

"He said his name was Tommy," Leslie later told the police. "He said he wanted to be my friend." But, like the black pistol Leslie pulled from the leather case in her desperate attempt to escape, the offer of friendship too was fake. The stranger did not want to be her friend and his name was not Tommy. He was called Jimmy in some places in New York, but his old friends called him Rich. His full name was Richard Francis Cottingham and his arrest by Patrolman Stanley Melowic on May 22, 1980, was just the beginning of the painfully meticulous work by detectives in New Jersey and New York City in closing the books on not one, but five murders, including the 1977 suffocation death of Maryann Carr.

*Four*

# The Solitary Suspect

Richard Cottingham lived in a quiet, residential neighborhood in a town of about 23,000 called Lodi in southern Bergen County, not far from Route 17 and about a half-hour drive from New York City. He and Janet, whom he'd married at Our Lady of Lourdes Church in Queens Village, New York, on May 3, 1970, rented a simple three-bedroom Cape Cod at 29 Vreeland Street, not far from the banks of the Saddle River. The Cottinghams stayed to themselves, neither wanting nor fitting the fabric of their new community. Janet had been brought up in New York. Richard was born in the Bronx in New York, but his family had moved from the city while he was still a youngster. They had settled in River Vale, a tiny village by comparison, where Richard enjoyed a boy's life in a community that was transforming from a rural farming town to a commuter, bedroom community.

Life in the suburbs of New York City can be a mixture of a search for happiness or, for some, just comfort, while longing to be where the action is. Janet Cottingham, who had borne three children in her ten-year marriage, was content to make a home for her family. She was happy living in the house on Vreeland Street, where they had moved in 1975. Her loneliness for her old neighborhood in Queens Village was helped somewhat by visits from high school friends and relatives. Janet liked the house far better than the two-bedroom apartment they had in nearby Little Ferry. The apartment had become impractical for the growing family. Blair, their oldest, was a toddler when Janet became pregnant with Scott, who was born in March of 1975, a month after the family moved into 29 Vreeland Street. Jenny, the couple's last child and only daughter, came along in October, 1976.

With three children born just three years apart, Janet had all the activity she wanted. But if one thing was lacking, it was more companionship from her husband. Their sex life, she couldn't argue, had been frequent and often satisfying for most of the first five years of their marriage, but Janet knew deep down that something had gone wrong. Like most housewives, she looked in the mirror for the cause. But it was after Jenny was born that her husband refused outright to come to her in bed when he arrived home after his job on the late shift. Janet, left alone with her thoughts while her husband spent most of his waking day away from their home, experienced the slow drain of marital trust and emotional security. These thoughts were fueled by the cumulative effect of his absences, but the compounding and overwhelming shock to an already fragile relationship would be dealt to Janet when she learned what her husband had been doing during his ventures away from home.

While Richard may also have been unhappy with the marriage, he had more than enough outside interests to compensate. And he was enjoying his two oldest children, Blair, who was seven on October 15, 1979, and Scott, who would turn five the following March 28. From outward apearances, the children were well taken care of and seemed healthy and happy. The infrequent times neighbors would see the children, they seemed to be the product of a happy home and a protective father. Janet dressed them in costumes for Halloween and Richard took the kids door-to-door to trick or treat. To neighbors, he was the doting, loving father, well aware of the uncertainties that could befall young children left alone on the streets at night.

The isolation of the family from the friendly neighborhood in Lodi and the extremely private nature of the head of the household at 29 Vreeland Street were acceptable characteristics in the strongly Italian community. The women of the community who knew of this relatively new family—most of Lodi's residents were natives or citizens of long-standing—could accept what might ordinarily be interpreted as unfriendliness as long as the children were cared for. The men respected a man's privacy and desire to protect his home. The fact that few people really got to know the Cottinghams in Lodi was, in a reverse sense, a sign that the family was law abiding and normal. At least that was the community's perception.

Being remote in a community and removed from the mainstream—difficult in today's society, what with the inter-dependence most people have come to rely on in American suburbia since World War II—is usually the trademark of an individualist or an eccentric. For those who knew Richard Cottingham as a friend, the sandy-haired computer programmer fits the description of an extremely shy individual, an underachiever who never really expressed his wants and needs. He was a participant by physical presence, but was never truly involved. If there was something he wanted, some fantasy he wished to act out, he did not express it, at least not in the boyhood atmosphere he knew when his parents, William and Anna Cottingham, brought him and his two sisters to live in Bergen County, New Jersey.

Moving to the suburbs was the upwardly mobile thing to do for William Cottingham, a quiet, almost brooding career man who had risen from a line sales position to the executive level at Metropolitan Life Insurance Company in New York. It was his turn now to take his family away from the congested and crime-infested atmosphere of Bronx, one of the five overpopulated boroughs that compose New York County. It was time for a new standard of life, one that would include a split-level house in the rustic New Jersey suburbs. River Vale, a community that was still divided between dairy farmers and briefcase toters in the 1960's, became home for the Cottingham family in 1958.

It was a confident age. The nation was at peace and Dwight Eisenhower was in the White House. It was before Soviet technolgy hurled Sputnik into outer space and well after the lads had come home from Korea. The national guilt had receded after the red scare and the death of Joseph McCarthy in 1957. Democrats and Republicans were going about the business of finding suitable candidates for the 1960 presidential election, while everyone else got down to living and making a living. For William Cottingham, it was off each day at the crack of dawn, brown suit and briefcase, for the walk to the bus station. Anna, like millions of other housewives made sure the children were dressed and fed and ready for school. For their oldest child and only son, Richard, the early morning meant a long bus ride to Westwood, where he was entered in the seventh grade at St. Andrews, a parochial school for boys and girls.

Richard Cottingham, who became known to his high school chums as Rich, had little difficulty with the discipline the nuns instilled at St. Andrews. But he did have trouble making friends. Partly due to the fact that the family was new to the area and because he was a commuting school child, Rich did not get to know many other kids in his neighborhood around the family's home on Cleveland Avenue in River Vale. As a result, he spent much of his time on weekends, holidays, and during the summer vacations working and tinkering around the house and yard with his mother.

He was not an athletic sort of child and his poor eyesight made sports difficult, particularly the more popular sports of baseball and football. When, like most boys of his age, he did develop an interest, it was not one that other youngsters could easily share. He didn't collect stamps or coins, nor did he pester his parents to buy him fishing gear. Young Richard took an interest in pigeons, homing pigeons. Again, it was a solitary kind of activity, not one that attracted the kids from the neighborhood.

He was a handsome boy and when he left Saint Andrews in 1960 and entered Pascack Valley High School in nearby Hillsdale, Rich became more accepted, or perhaps more acceptable. Pascack Valley was one of those regional secondary schools built to meet the necessity brought about by the post-World-War-II baby boom. The kids who went there had no roots in a community, because they came from towns like River Vale that either couldn't afford to build high schools or didn't have enough teenaged kids to make it practical. Nevertheless, Rich was no longer an outsider, even if he did still nurture a Bronx accent. He became part of an age group looking for identity.

The high school itself, founded only five years before he was enrolled, was searching for prestige. Almost to a boy, the male students seemed to aim for the same thing and Pascack Valley sought to prove that kids from the hilly, farm towns of western Bergen County could produce an athletic program that would prove them to be a power to reckon with. Rich Cottingham's contribution was to join the cross country and track teams, activity that required endurance, not good eyes. A slender kid, with unruly blond hair, Cottingham picked the event that most fit his personality. He chose the solitude and loneliness of the long distance runner. From that time and until his graduation in 1964, Rich Cottingham established the pace he would hold through his adult life.

He was not one of the hoods who only cared about hot cars; he was not one of the scholarly types who made the National Honor Society and got elected to the student council; and he was not one of the jocks who earned two or three varsity letters and had the cheerleaders in tow at all the high school dances. "The only thing I never understood about Rich was that he looked like a hood, but he ran track. He was sort of a bridge between the hoods and the jocks. But everyone did strange things in high school, and he was no stranger than anyone else," recalled one of Rich's high school chums. Kids in the class of 1964 at Pascack Valley remembered one other detail about Cottingham, perhaps one that answered the question of why he just didn't want to fit in. He was never a star, just one in the crowd. And he never seemed to show up for yearbook pictures.

Once he was out of high school, Cottingham began to exert himself as an individual in his own family. He hadn't achieved the kind of grade average that would impress college admission officials, nor did he particularly care to pursue more schooling, but his father wanted Rich to start in at a career. It was either that, or he would end up in the military, but that was an avenue Cottingham, helped by poor eyesight, managed to avoid altogether. William Cottingham arranged to have his son hired by Metropolitan Life in the insurance giant's computer center in New York. Rich worked as a computer operator and took courses to learn more about the technology. He came to like the work and the income, even if the night hours were inconvenient.

Then came Rich's first decision that had to upset his father. He took the knowledge of computers he had absorbed in the eighteen months with Metropolitan Life and joined another firm that had offered him more money. He started with Blue Cross and Blue Shield of Greater New York in 1966. Showing consistency and a desire for advancement, he gradually moved up the ladder at Blue Cross, which employed about 200 people in its computer center on Third Avenue, between 40th and 41st streets on Manhattan's East Side. Cottingham moved with the company when it left its old Lexington Avenue location in 1975. Still living at home and free to go his own way when he wasn't working, Rich was happy during his first years with Blue Cross, or at least that's what he told his old high school friends. Like his father, he learned to live with the bus ride into and out of Manhattan each workday.

*Five*

# The Trophy Room

The arrest made by Patrolman Stan Melowic in Hasbrouck Heights, New Jersey, on the morning of May 22, 1980, would have repercussions across the country. Police queries came in from Los Angeles, Las Vegas, Maryland, and Delaware. Detectives in those areas had cases in which women had been abducted, raped, murdered, and mutilated. Authorities in Los Angeles were especially interested in any similarities between the crimes investigated in New Jersey and New York. The previous June, two young prostitutes, ages fifteen and twenty-one, were discovered in a deserted industrial site. Their heads, hands, and feet had been cut off. They apeared to have been bound or restrained in some manner. The jewelry they were said to have been wearing when least seen together was missing from the mutilated bodies. The police agencies in these various jurisdictions were looking for a similar method of procedure, or modus operandi. Beyond the lurid details of the crimes, a similar m.o. might be traced to a man who handcuffed or tied his victims, did his thing, and then—and this was the part that intrigued detectives—stole some item of personal value. It was like a trophy awarded for a great deed, or, in this instance, a monstrous one.

New Jersey and New York authorities, though just a wide body of water apart, rarely worked together. Even back in the heyday of Murder Inc., when New York mobsters routinely silenced their rivals or enemies and discarded the remains in New Jersey's swamplands, cooperation was rare. The poor relations and disrespect went back further, to the Lindbergh kidnapping in 1932, when the investigation focused on Bruno Hauptmann, an obscure carpenter from the Bronx. The New Jersey State Police jealously guarded information from their investigation of the kidnapping; the District Attorney of the Bronx conducted his own grand jury probe of the Hauptmann gang. Back in New Jersey, where the Lindbergh baby had been scooped from his cradle and killed in a fall from the escape ladder, a Princeton University president begged law enforcement agencies to "unite to get the persons who have done this thing." It was in no small degree due to the bitter rivalry between the two police networks, unmitigated by the powerlessness of the Federal Bureau of Investigation, that kidnapping was made a federal crime not long after the abduction of twenty-month-old Charles Augustus Lindbergh, Jr.

But if political boundaries still kept them from joining in any kind of efficient relationship, the police networks in New York and New Jersey did establish some friendly ties in time to aid the investigation into who was abducting and brutalizing young hookers from Manhattan's street market. It was detectives like Tony Tortora, Richard Ruffino, and Larry Garafolo, all assigned to the missing persons bureau of the Bergen County Sheriff's Department; and some others like Jimmy Kean, Gerald McQueen, Michael Clark, Edward Dahlem, Anthony Oricoli, and Richard Bohan from police precincts in Manhattan—all career professionals—who helped restore the law enforcement unity that distrust and disrespect had shattered over the years.

Anthony Tortora, a short, stocky man with an easy smile, had worked the four to midnight shift May 16 at the missing persons bureau, where he was an investigator. Because of its reputation for dogged determination and its successes with other cases, the bureau had been assigned to the task of finding out the true identity of the young woman who was found strangled inside Room 132 at the Quality Inn. There wasn't much to go on. All the woman was wearing when her body was discovered the morning of May 4 were a pair of metal handcuffs and some adhesive tape fastened tightly to her mouth. A photograph and her description indicated only that a woman in her early twenties, possibly younger, with light blue eyes, strawberry blond hair, who went by the name of Shelly Dudley, had been found murdered. The photograph of her five-foot-four-inch, 137-pound body showed severe bruises to the face and neck. A two-inch scar on the left elbow was the only distinguishing mark except for the stretch marks around her abdomen, which indicated a weight loss, possibly from an abortion or childbirth. Following the basic procedures used in cases of missing persons reports, Detective Tortora distributed the photograph to police agencies in New Jersey, and he also provided copies to the public morals squad in New York, headquartered at 138 West 30th Street in Mid-Manhattan West precinct.

The pimp squad, as New York City's public morals division was known, had its office in a dimly lit room above police headquarters in the building between Sixth and Seventh Avenues. It was an appropriate location, a spot providing a good vantage point to Manhattan's sleazy hotels and rundown commercial district. About the only bright spot in the World War II vintage offices was Karen Kritzan, a bright young detective who had been assigned to Inspector Anthony Ciccotelli's division for about two years. Krizan was a street wise cop who had no trouble fitting in with the veterans of Mid-Manhattan West, particularly after her undercover work as a masseuse at the Gramercy Leisure Spa on Manhattan's posh East Side brought the conviction of the sex palace's operator and three cohorts.

Members of the pimp squad had worked in conjunction with the task force on the Times Square torso murders; some squad members were also asked to assist on the investigation of the mutilation murder of Jean Reyner at the Hotel Seville on May 15. Their knowledge was invaluable since all three murder victims were prostitutes. Because Bergen County detectives suspected that Shelly Dudley was also a prostitute, it was natural for Investigator Tortora to call on his friend Jimmy Kean at the pimp squad for assistance.

Detective Kean was on the graveyard shift the day after the Hotel Seville murder. He was handling the routine complaints and paper work on a minor arrest of a prostitute named Diana, a young hooker who happened to be on the wrong corner at the right time for a sweep of arrests by the pimp squad. She told Kean that her pimp had taken off, possibly for Philadelphia, and she was alone since her girlfriend, the one who had shared a room with her, had been missing. Kean's eyes lit up as he reached for the photograph of Shelly Dudley.

Detective Tortora had gotten off his shift only two hours before and was barely asleep when the telephone rang at his home in Bergen County. It didn't take him long to dress and make the drive across the bridge and down the Henry Hudson Parkway to West 30th Street. He was in Kean's office within forty-five minutes of the call. Diana was sitting on a bench in the hallway, sobbing between drags on a cigarette. Jimmy Kean related to Tortora how the girl had broken into tears when she saw the photo of Shelly Dudley, the one with the ugly bruise over the right eye. "That's my girlfriend Valorie," she said with a whimper, telling the two detectives she had dyed her girlfriend's natural brown hair the color in the picture, strawberry blond.

The hooker told Tortora that Valorie had spoken of her mother and a sister who live outside Miami, in a place called Leisure City. Tortora rechecked his contacts in Dade County, Florida. Valorie or Shelly Dudley meant nothing, no record of such a person in Miami or Leisure City. But within the next few days, Tortora had dispatched a set of prints taken from the murder victim. Word came back. A nineteen-year-old woman named Valorie Ann Street had once been arrested by Miami police and was jailed for a week on a charge of soliciting for the purpose of prostitution. Yes, she had one distinguishing mark on her body, the Miami report said, a slight, two-inch scar on the left elbow. The silent victim had finally spoken.

Valorie Ann Street, a young woman who had only just blossomed into adolescence, was from Indiana, the child of a steelworker from Gary. Valorie, like Leslie O'Dell, was running away from something. For Leslie, it had been an angry fight with her boyfriend. Valorie Street was running from the law. Both women had arrived in New York City well after the bizarre, decapitation murders at the Travel Inn on 42nd Street, the infamous torso murders that were discovered December 2, 1979. Valorie had arrived in New York City in early May, 1980—too early to hear the warning about another hooker, Jean Reyner, whose body was found, stabbed and strangled, breasts surgically removed, at the Hotel Seville on May 15, 1980. Valorie Street was getting away from Miami because she had become too well known after her arrest in that city on a prostitution charge. That was April 15. Two weeks later she was in New York, rooming with the hooker named Diana. Four days after that she was dead.

Valorie was last seen in Manhattan in the early morning hours of May 4, a Sunday, working the streets off Madison Avenue on the East Side, between 30th and 35th Streets. She was wearing a simple, white blouse and jeans, with dirty white tennis shoes on her feet. It was after three in the morning when Valorie, using the name Shelly Dudley, signed herself in at the Quality Inn Motel in New Jersey. The clerk gave her the key to Room 132 and that was the last time anyone saw her alive; anyone, that is, but the man who strangled her and stuffed her nude body under the motel room bed.

Since Valorie couldn't tell of her torture, the scientific, medical, and criminal laboratory reports had to speak for her. It was, according to a medical examiner's opinion, a six- to twenty-four-hour ordeal for Valorie Street in Room 132. The screams that brought help for Leslie O'Dell were unheard from Valorie's mouth, which had been tightly sealed with adhesive tape. She had eaten a short time before her death, but the food had aparently failed to weaken the alcohol or drugs that took hold of her body. The tests showed Valorie was quite intoxicated, possibly drugged. Such a state, the prosecutor, Dennis Calo, would later conclude, made it impossible for Valorie to defend herself from the severe beating she took to the face and head, the savage bitings that caused her nipples to bleed, the forced anal and vaginal rape that left evidence of a painful and prolonged sexual attack, and the deep ligature around the right side of her neck that told detectives she was strangled to death.

The murderer took great precautions to cover his tracks to Room 132. All of Valorie's belongings, right down to her panties, were removed. The sheets, which might have had a trace of semen, were removed from the bed, as was the other bedding. The police thoroughly dusted for fingerprints and vacuumed the carpet to detect the presence of any foreign fibers or human hairs. The only undeniable clue was the cheap pair of Japanese manufactured handcuffs that bound Valorie's hands behind her back as she endured her sadistic punishment.

The Valorie Street investigation had two immediate tasks: a background had to be done on Valorie Street to determine if anyone saw her approached by a man driving a New Jersey licensed vehicle the morning of May 4; and the fingerprint people in Bergen County had to find if the fingerprints of anyone with an arrest record, or if anyone who had ever had reason to be fingerprinted for a gun permit or for military service, might match the prints taken from the handcuffs found on Valorie. It was not much, but the investigation finally had a focus, if not a suspect.

Criminologists have made exhaustive studies of certain behavioral patterns among criminals. One type of pattern that has always intrigued professionals, including police psychiatrists, is that left by the trademark criminal. A pattern that includes a trademark is usually either the mark of a contract killer or the symbol of a homicidal maniac. In either instance, the murderer wants credit for the homicide. The professional killer will often use a specific weapon and leave the victim with a fatal wound to a certain part of the body. The trademark is proof to his employer that the target was hit and final payment is deserved. The New York metropolitan area has seen a series of 22-caliber pistol murders, which have usually been found related to the illicit drug market and can generally be attributed to a single gang that uses the small-caliber weapon for its ease of handling and reliability.

The homicidal maniac is seeking payment of a far different value for his or her deeds. But the result, with some infrequent variation, is often the same as regards a trademark. Albert H. De Salvo had two basic methods that became his trademark in the strangulation murders of thirteen women in and around Boston between 1962 and 1964. De Salvo, who chose female targets whether they were senior citizens or teenaged women, would gain entry to the victim's home by posing as a plumber or handyman, usually sent by the building superintendent. But the constant sign that got him national attention as the Boston Strangler was De Salvo's technique with the stocking or cord he used to choke the oxygen from the victim's lungs. It was always a bow-like knot De Salvo tied around the necks of the women he murdered.

Besides the Maryann Carr case and other unsolved murders of two teenaged girls whose nude and sexually tortured bodies had been found in a wooded lot on August 15, 1974, their hands and feet tightly bound before they were suffocated, the police in Bergen County reviewed four other cases during the Valorie Street murder investigation. These four were not murders, but they were sexual attacks on young women whose bodies had been beaten or tortured. Three of the women, including Leslie Ann O'Dell, were prostitutes, the third was a twenty-two-year-old New Jersey housewife who was working as a waitress in New York at the time of her abduction. The housewife and one of the other women were pregnant at the time of their confrontation with the man who would ultimately be charged and convicted of the murder of Valorie Street. The single and most extraordinary similarity between the three abductions and sexual attacks was that each of the women claimed to have been robbed of some personal belonging.

For Karen Schilt, it began over a friendly drink at a little bar on Third Avenue in New York, not far from Bellevue Hospital, where she had been visiting her hospitalized husband. Although she would later refer to September 23, 1978, as "a night I'll never forget," Karen spent most of the time of her abduction and sexual abuse in a drugged stupor. She was found early the next morning lying in a sewer, robbed of her coat, purse, and a silver ring. She spent several days in a hospital in Hackensack, the first five hours in an unconscious state.

Susan Geiger, a nineteen-year-old blonde from Florida, was soliciting between Broadway and Seventh Avenue on 47th Street near the Capitol Hotel when she met "this guy" and made a "date" to meet him the following night, October 12, 1978, at the Americana Hotel. They met for drinks at the hotel and moved on to another bar. The next clear thing Susan remembered was waking up to find this man beating her with a rubber hose. When she finally came out of a drugged trance, she was lying on the floor of a motel room in South Hackensack, New Jersey. She was nude and in severe pain, bleeding from her mouth, breasts, vagina, and rectum. To add insult to injury, Susan was robbed of her earrings, clothing and her purse.

Pamela Weisenfeld, a twenty-seven-year-old hooker who also claimed to do some school teaching during the week, met the man on May 11, 1980. Her story had a similar ring to those of Karen and Susan and her case was included in an indictment voted by a Bergen County grand jury in September of 1980. Pamela claimed she was drugged, beaten, and savagely bitten on the breasts. She woke up in a vacant lot in Teaneck, New Jersey, robbed of her purse and jewelry.

The robberies were important to the cases Bergen County authorities would press before the grand jury and ultimately to a twelve-member jury that heard the trial of Richard F. Cottingham; but to New Jersey investigators, the handcuffs were the most important trademark of their suspect during the more than four-month investigation of Valorie Street's murder. To New York City authorities, who had three mutilation murder cases to close, the robberies of clothing, jewelry, and other personal belongings were of major significance. The significance of that kind of trademark would suggest a pattern, a pattern wherein the murderer tortured his victims before taking their lives and then took something else with him. It was a final act that strongly pointed to the possiblity that the suspect would be a collector of trophies or tokens. One leading psychologist advised that this trademark might have a fetishistic element, while a noted psychiatrist speculated that the taking of a victim's clothing or personal belongings, like jewelry, suggested the assailant wanted to take possession of the victim.

Janet Cottingham was bewildered by all the commotion of May 22, 1980. First she got the telephone call from the Hasbrouck Heights police, telling her that her husband was under arrest. Next, about a dozen detectives converged on her home at 29 Vreeland Street. Janet, a pleasant, reasonably attractive woman who appeared somewhat older than her thirty years, had good reason to be distraught that day. In searching the house, detectives had found a collection of mysterious items in a room in the basement of the Cottingham home. As the items were brought out and placed on a table for inspection and identification, the detectives began asking her questions. Where did the clothing, the jewelry, the perfume, the motel keys, the purses—where did all these women's items come from? Janet appeared apprehensive. She said, at one point, when some bottles of perfume were brought to her attention, that perhaps some of the items were bought as gifts for her. After all she had been through, Janet maintained a certain protective resistance to telling these men her true feelings. It must have been extremely painful to admit that on their tenth anniversary, May 3, the day before Valorie Street was murdered, her husband went to work and then stayed out until the early morning of May 4.

Janet finally broke down. She conceded that with his work shift and unpredictable schedule before and after work, she couldn't be sure exactly when her husband was home. One detective thought that this was a woman who was suppressing as much pain as any knowledge she might have, but he concluded that she probably knew very little. After all, she wasn't even allowed in the locked basement room of her own home. That was Richard Cottingham's exclusive domain, what some policemen would begin to call his "Trophy Room."

# *Six*

# After the First Week, It Was Downhill

At the same time police detectives were questioning his wife and tagging the female items stored in the isolated basement room in the couple's home in Lodi, Richard Cottingham sat alone in a cell at the Hasbrouck Heights police station. He was in a hell of a jam and he knew it. But Richard was not the type to allow consternation to show on his face. Quietly shy, almost an introvert by nature, he appeared stoic, holding what he knew and felt inside. He was not a fool. He would tell them nothing.

But, in other ways, Cottingham had already provided detectives with ample information. In that simple statement, blurted to Patrolman Melowic, Cottingham had let the police know that he had reason to be scared. He was with a hooker, Leslie Ann O'Dell. Okay, with that admission he could join thousands of other men who turn to prostitutes for sex or any of a dozen other reasons. He got scared, Cottingham had said in his moment of fear. Why? He hadn't done anything, his simple statement said. Nobody, including Patrolman Melowic, had asked if he could explain, just after his mad dash from Room 117, why he was running. Those were his own words, according to the policeman and others who were in earshot. Then there are the other incidentals and items. Among the things he was carrying were a pistol, which turned out to be a cheap toy, and a black-handled knife with a three-inch blade. In the black leather case he had in one hand were found three sets of handcuffs, several containers of pills, a black leather mouth gag, and two black leather slave collars with bright chrome studs. And last, but not least, Cottingham had in his jacket pocket a key for Room 117. It was one of those occasions when the less said, the worse matters appeared. Yes, he was under arrest for attacking and attempting to murder the O'Dell woman and it was a real jam. But that was only the beginning.

Detective Edward Denning and the other investigators were beginning to ask questions about other crimes. Just days after Cottingham's May 22 arrest, detectives interviewed Karen Schilt, the housewife who was abducted from New York City and left off at an apartment complex in Little Ferry. It was the Ledgewood Terrace apartments, where the Cottinghams had lived until 1975. It was also the same complex where Maryann Carr and her husband Michael had an apartment in 1977. Maryann was last seen alive outside her apartment building, talking to a man who appeared to have the same physical dimensions as her husband, but Michael Carr had been in New York State on business December 15. His wife's body was discovered the following day outside the Quality Inn.

Cottingham insisted that he had never been to the Quality Inn before he registered there as a guest with Leslie Ann O'Dell. But another woman, a New York City nurse he had dated back in 1977, would tell detectives that she shared a room at the motel with Cottingham on at least two occasions in the summer of 1977 and the fall of 1978. The nurse friend was Barbara Lucas. She also told police that Richard also liked to be called Blair and that he was known in a few Manhattan bars as Jimmy. She said Richard's favorite hangout was Flanagan's on First Avenue, where Susan Geiger had a few drinks with Cottingham before he took her to another New Jersey motel for her night of torture.

If Cottingham was thinking of what events in his life might be investigated because of his attack on Leslie Ann O'Dell, he certainly wasn't telling the police. But the pressure from the one case alone was intense. As he spent those solitary moments in that cramped space of the Hasbrouck Heights jail cell, Richard fidgeted with his glasses. He'd been forced to wear them since he was just a boy of nine and he had always hated the embarassment he felt while wearing them. In a moment of total desperation, he smashed the wire-rim glasses on the floor, picked up a sliver of glass and cut into his left wrist. The blood spewed over his clothes and onto the floor. But the suicide attempt was quickly aborted when a policeman assigned to keep watch noticed the blood. Cottingham was rushed to the county's hospital in Paramus, treated for the cut and transferred to the Bergen County Jail.

The next day, May 23, Cottingham appeared for his arraignment on the charge of attempted murder of eighteen-year-old Leslie O'Dell. Bail was set at $250,000, a high amount for a first-time offender. But Prosecutor Dennis Calo, a brash young attorney who would press the state's case against Cottingham, persuaded the judge that the defendant "had a bad reputation and inclinations of criminal activity." The judge, Benedict E. Lucchi of New Jersey's Superior court bench, rejected the pleas of Wakeley Paul, Cottingham's hastily appointed attorney, who complained about the high amount of the bail. Paul noted Cottingham's consistent employment and his support of a wife and three children. Judge Lucchi also dismissed Paul's other argument, that if, as the prosecutor was suggesting, there was trouble with Cottingham's mental condition, then the prosecutor "ought to offer psychiatric evaluation." There was no question of the fact that the thirty-three-year-old defendant had been treated *only* for his lacerated wrist at

Bergen Pines County Hospital, an institution with a full-time staff of psychologists and psychiatrists. The suicide attempt was forgotten long before the defendant's wrist would heal.

The news of Richard Cottingham's arrest was received with measured relief from New York's streetwalkers and hotel hookers. It reached them through word-of-mouth and the media, which had jumped on the double mutilation murder of the two prostitutes at the end of 1979 and brought the bizarre case back to life when Jean Reyner's body was discovered May 15, seven days before Cottingham was caught. "I felt relieved a little bit," said Jennifer, a tall, willowy blonde who used to ply her trade at the motel where the two girls were decapitated. "But you never know," she cautiously added, "there are a lot of lunatics running around New York."

But while there was cautious relief on the streets, the New York City Police Department was jubilant. Finally they had a suspect they could work with, even if he was being held in a New Jersey jail. There was a great deal of rehashing and new legwork to be done, but the Times Square task force, directed by Sergeant Gerald McQueen, and Sergeant Edward Dahlem's squad from the Thirteenth Precinct, investigating Jean Reyner's murder at the Hotel Seville, were suddenly able to focus on a case that no longer seemed hopeless. And all because the guy who became their prime suspect was stupid enough to be caught coming out of a motel room after almost killing another prostitute.

Paul Beakmon, who was still assigned to the December 1979 torso murders, was certain of one thing. The stranger who signed the Travel Inn Motor Hotel register as Carl Wilson was from New Jersey. Otherwise, why would he make up an address of Anderson Place, Merlin, New Jersey, when he checked in on November 29. Bolstered by his conviction that the same man was responsible for the prostitute attacks he investigated back in 1973 and 1974, Beakmon was one of several investigators who pressed extra hard to shut this case. He felt strongly that a handwriting analysis would confirm his hunch. Beakmon had seen several suspects whose handwriting was studied and compared to the mythical Carl Wilson's, and because he had that gut feeling that the visitor to Room 417 of the Travel Inn was his man, the detective was secretly happy the others were eliminated during the more than five months he had spent investigating the double murder. Beakmon was exuberant when he heard that the District Attorney's office was moving to get a handwriting sample from Richard Cottingham.

Sergeant Edward Dahlem knew that Jean Reyner, the twenty-five-year-old hooker whose breasts were removed and body set on fire after she was strangled in Room 1139 of the Hotel Seville, was a high-class prostitute. Jean, whose age was probably more like thirty-four, if you considered her long arrest record on prostitution offenses, liked to dress well and wear expensive jewelry. Dahlem never could understand why she ended her career at the Seville. It just wasn't her caliber place to work. But he was certain that her body, found sprawled on the floor near the door of the partially burned hotel room, had jewelry on it before she was strangled. If they found the person or persons who committed the murder, his detectives might also find that jewelry. It wasn't in the room or the hotel and the firemen sure as hell wouldn't dare take it, the detective mused, especially with a murder investigation in the offing. If this guy in New Jersey was checked out, they might find that he either kept the stuff or fenced it somewhere.

The torso murders task force began working with authorities in the Bergen County prosecutor's office. But they still had some work to do on their own. Now that a New Jersey resident was the prime suspect, they had some other searching to continue. There was still the outstanding answer on where the murderer took those heads and hands he so carefully removed from the two girls at the Travel Inn. It was a thankless task, one that had taken task force investigators through delapidated docks and warehouses along the west side, on the banks of the Hudson River. Garbage had been sifted, incinerators checked for bones, even the manholes that lead to the massive underworld of New York's sewer lines were searched. There had been no trace of the heads and hands of

Deedeh Goodarzi and her partner victim in the Times Square torso murders. The prospect of what anyone would do with such a quarry sent chills up the spine of one black prostitute, who was relieved with the knowledge that the New Jersey suspect usually chose white women for his prey. "What was he doing with all those parts?" she asked out loud. "Was he goin' home and rubbin' himself with them?"

Members of the Times Square task force were sent out to New Jersey and told to search possible dump sites. But if the parts were stuck in a plastic bag meant for the garbage trucks that make daily trips to the meadowlands, northern New Jersey's major dump, the detectives might as well quit. The meadowlands takes in enough garbage each day to fill New York's Yankee Stadium. The investigation was well into the sixth month, which would mean excavating tons of debris over miles of the rancid mountains of trash. They might as well be looking for the remains of Jimmy Hoffa, the slain Teamster Union leader whose body was thought to have ended up in a trash compactor in nearby Hudson County, New Jersey. The primary reason New York wanted to collect the remains of the two women was identity. They knew who one of the victims was, but the other girl's name remained a mystery. Miss Goodarzi's partner, a white female of about twenty, was known only as New York Medical Examiner's Case Number 79-8105. After several days of fruitlessly searching New Jersey dumps, the task force decided it best to concentrate on the suspect. He might be the only person who could lead them to the victims' parts.

Since neither New York nor New Jersey had an indictment against Cottingham, outside observers began to see the dual but separate probes as a race between murder investigators. Bergen County was holding the sandy-haired computer operator for the attempted murder of Leslie Ann O'Dell, but legal observers and news reporters speculated that the jurisdiction with the strongest case would finally send Cottingham to trial. Roger Breslin's staff at the Bergen County prosecutor's office was working day and night on the Valorie Street murder and several other new and old cases. Progress was slow and expensive. After two months, the office had run up nearly $30,000 in overtime pay, much of it paid to the two dozen investigators, lawyers, and technical staff working to present evidence before a county grand jury. The substantial difference between the resources of the two agencies was that the investigation in New York, under the ultimate responsibility of District Attorney Robert M. Morgenthau, was one of more than a thousand, whereas Bergen County was working at the time on a total caseload of fifteen homicide investigations.

The two probes basically came down to focus on three crucial pieces of evidence: eyewitness accounts and identification of the defendant; assorted items of jewelry and female belongings taken by search warrant from Richard Cottingham's basement; and, perhaps most incriminating, the signature of the murderer on motel registration records and on his tools of torture, the latter being the prints found on the handcuffs that shackled Valorie Street until her death on May 4. New York had struck out with eyewitnesses, but Nancy Ryan, Morgenthau's young assistant district attorney in charge of presenting the office's three murder cases to a Manhattan grand jury, asserted that the grand jury was convinced by other evidence. In a hastily called news conference on August 14, 1980, Morgenthau announced a three-count indictment against Richard Cottingham. But even with the mutilation murder indictments, New York could only serve Cottingham with the arrest warrants. He remained in Breslin's custody, his bail now raised to $350,000. Morgenthau's office said New York did not have to wait to begin with extradition proceedings to bring Cottingham to trial, but wait they did.

Anna Cottingham, a prim woman whose sandy blond hair had taken on the natural grey strains suited to her sixty-two years of age, reacted to the charges against her son with bitter outrage. She and Richard, her oldest child, had a close, perhaps unusually sensitive, relationship when Richard was growing up in River Vale.

She had reacted angrily before when her son was taken away from her—when he chose to marry Janet in 1970. Then the newly wed couple decided to stay in New Jersey rather than move with the family to Florida. Now he was being taken away from her again.

The charges were unbelievable to Anna. To Mrs. Cottingham, who had lost track of her son's daily habits and likes and dislikes, Richard was still the young, solitary boy who liked pigeons more than anything else. But Anna, quietly conservative, let the younger members of her family do the talking in Richard's defense. The mother would do all a mother could do; she hired the best known defense attorney her money could buy. And that is why she had chosen Donald Conway. After all, he was a former president of the Bar Association in New Jersey. He was a trial lawyer with an excellent reputation for defending his clients, no matter who they were or what they had been accused of doing. Anna had made the arrangements to hire Conway soon after Richard was locked away in the Bergen County Jail. Ultimately, she would have to put her home in Tampa up for sale to pay the bill, but Anna Cottingham never relented. In her heart, she knew that Richard was innocent.

It was little more than a month after the New York triple murder indictment that New Jersey officially put its case on the line for a vote by the twenty-two grand jury members who had reviewed the evidence against Richard Cottingham. And their answer was a resounding affirmation of the police work that reached far and wide to gather up evidence of brutal attacks on four women and the murder of two others. When the grand jury had completed its deliberation on September 17, 1980, it had approved a 21-count indictment. The laundry list included every sadistic act in the book: carnal knowledge (rape); atrocious assault (cutting, beating, biting); aggravated assault (attempting to cause serious bodily harm); aggravated sexual assault while armed (rape, sodomy, fellatio); attempted murder (by purposely strangling, suffocating, assaulting, and cutting with a knife). And there were the drug charges. Cottingham was charged with possession of Diazepam, Secobarbit, and Amobarbital, which are tranquilizers and barbituates and were among the items he was carrying when he left Leslie Ann O'Dell at the Quality Inn. The story of three of the women who had been abducted in New York and left off in either a motel or out on some abandoned street was that they were drugged by Cottingham. The prosecutors purposely put the drug charges in the bill before the grand jury to bolster the women's stories.

To support his case, Dennis Calo, the assistant prosecutor in charge of the county homicide bureau, promised eyewitness accounts from four of the victims. Leslie Ann O'Dell, Susan Geiger, and Karen Schilt had all identified Cottingham in police lineups. Pamela Weisenfeld, a twenty-seven-year-old prostitute who claimed she was abducted by the same man on May 12, 1980, would prove to be a troublesome witness for the state. Nevertheless, the grand jury had included a charge of kidnapping with regard to Pamela.

But the strongest evidence came through the silent victim, Valorie Street. Detective Robert S. Rehberg, an investigator for the county prosecutor's office, and laboratory technicians with the Federal Bureau of Investigation were able to match fingerprints lifted from the handcuffs used on Valorie with prints found on the cuffs around Leslie's hands when she was found alive in Room 117. As Calo would say, "Richard Cottingham left one thing in that room with Valorie Street." It was what criminologists call a latent fingerprint, or very light, old print, but only one person could have left it. The print, Prosecutor Calo would later declare, would allow one of Cottingham's silenced victims, Valorie Street, to talk.

The charges against Cottingham created a sensation. All the New Jersey newspapers carried the story and New York's media, always thirsty for news from the Garden State, leaped all over the story with camera and pen. With the stories came errors. Not that anyone really noticed or cared if they did make mistakes. One newspaper, well known for its careful reporting of New York police news, reported how the then thirty-three-year-old New Jersey man was the leading suspect in three mutilation murders in Manhattan and "a suspect in a string of sex attacks and mutilation slayings in

New Jersey." It then went on to point out that two murders, both by strangulation, the female victims' bodies found intact, were actually tied to Cottingham. *The Record* of Hackensack, New Jersey, created the most furor, however, when it printed an article on August 15, the day after the New York indictment was announced, which was entitled, "Defendant in Prostitutes' Killings an Enigma." The Bergen County Bar Association, describing the article as "cheap" [and] sensationalistic," accused the newspaper of overstepping the bounds of a free press with a "seriously prejudicial attack upon an individual who has not yet even been charged." What the Bar Association failed to realize in its consideration of the depth of detail in the article, is that the story was based on a thorough research of the state's case against Richard Cottingham. It was only after the review of the police investigation that the article confirmed that Cottingham faced a very strong case for prosecution. A senior editor correctly advised the Bar Association that the newspaper, however, retained greater faith that the case against Cottingham would be decided on its merits, not the pretrial publicity.

After his indictment for the New Jersey crimes, the months grew long and cold for Richard Cottingham in his quarters inside "the Bastille." The old Bergen County Jail, adjacent to the county courthouse in the center of Hackensack, resembles a fortress, with an ancient tower like the Bastille in Paris. The love affair between the press and this sensational murder suspect grew as cold as the weather outside. But not everyone stopped loving the lonely suspect. About the only thing that happened during this pretrial period to raise his morale was the decision by his wife to withdraw her suit for divorce. She simply told the court she was withdrawing the divorce proceedings "for my own reasons." Janet Cottingham did not visit her husband, however. She and the couple's three children relocated to a small apartment in Poughkeepsie, New York, about thirty miles north of Hackensack.

Richard's daily routine was one of constant flux inside the jail. Sheriff Joseph Job, who complained frequently that the old building should have been torn down or renovated, was highly concerned with security. He didn't like murder defendants in his jail: too much temptation to escape. He ordered that Cottingham be moved to a different cell each day, the idea being that the defendant wouldn't become too familiar with his surroundings. And on a bitter cold weekend in January, the sheriff's fears were confirmed. An inmate who had once escaped from the county's medium security annex had been caught trying to hacksaw his way out of the maximum security "Bastille." Sheriff Job said five of his officers had information that Cottingham had been taking part in the escape plan. But the hacksaw was confiscated and the plan aborted. The sheriff ordered a closer watch placed on the murder defendant.

During the long winter of his confinement, Cottingham did manage to walk out of the Bergen County Jail one time. He was taken to the New Jersey-run Adult Diagnostic and Treatment Center in Avenel, located in the central part of the state. Cottingham was evaluated by a team of psychologists and psychiatrists; the prosecution wanted a professional opinion on Cottingham's sadistic tendencies. Defense attorney Conway allowed for the state to have his client evaluated at the Avenel center because the doctors' findings might prove to be a strong defense on the ground of sexual deviance. Avenel, after all, was the state institution for the treatment of child molesters and those convicted on multiple rape offenses.

The defense of Richard Cottingham in one of the most gruesome criminal escapades in New Jersey history was becoming apparent. Conway would have him plead innocent and fight the merits of an overhwelming case for the prosecution. By March of 1981, the major motions promised by Cottingham's lawyers were meant only to defuse the enormous pretrial publicity, particularly in Bergen County. Conway would ask Judge Paul R. Huot, the Superior Court judge assigned to hear the trial, if he would sequester the jury. Huot denied the motion. Next, Cottingham's defense asked for a change of venue for the trial to a different county. Request denied. And finally, in a motion that is rarely granted, Conway moved to have the court bring in a foreign jury; in other words empanel jurors from outside of Bergen County and have them hear the trial in Hackensack. Judge Huot once again denied the motion, asserting that Cottingham could receive a fair and impartial hearing from his peers, his neighbors in Bergen County.

Conway did have one pretrial victory. Judge Huot ordered that the tenth count of the 21-count indictment be severed for a separate trial. The Maryann Carr murder, the judge decided, would be heard later. It was a severe blow to Prosecutor Dennis Calo's case, as he would readily admit. It was also a blow to a few courthouse wags who had chosen to call Cottingham's murder cases the "Street Carr murders."

# *Seven*

# You May Be Tempted to Flinch

"You may be tempted to flinch," Dennis Calo warned the jury of nine men and nine women (twelve jurors and six alternates). "The facts of this case are not pleasant," the thirty-three-year-old prosecutor asserted. "They are hard, they are bloody, and they are gruesome." It was May 19, almost a solid twelve months since Richard Francis Cottingham, formerly an unknown computer programmer from Lodi, had been locked up for the attempted murder of Leslie Ann O'Dell. Now O'Dell and three other women were to have their turn at justice. And Dennis Calo, a no nonsense lawyer who had been preparing for this day for nearly a year, wasn't going to disappoint those victims. Calo told the jury they would need three things to judge the facts: stamina, intelligence, and courage. "The courage not to flinch from the gruesome facts as they weave a picture of unspeakably cruel criminal activity."

The eighteen jurors, two of them twenty-year-old women, soon knew what the prosecutor meant, as Calo read off the victims' names and shouted; "He kidnapped, in some cases drugged, beat, burned, raped, and sodomized them." And then there was Valorie Street, Calo screamed, nearly drowning out defense attorney Conway's objection to the prosecutor's tactics of overkill and Judge Huot's decision to overrule. "She is the one that Richard Cottingham killed." The evidence will show, he said, that Richard Cottingham was the man who locked Valorie Street in handcuffs, "beat her, and tortured her, and finally he strangled her in his strange ritual of sex and violence."

It was the kind of opening statement that is patently made for writers of juicy newspaper headlines. And one newspaper covering the trial verified this by topping its next day's article with, "Prosecutor Paints Cottingham Modern Day Ripper." The headline alone nearly caused Judge Huot to lock the jury away in a motel in sequestration. But the press was not the villain that caused the next bizarre set of events. The reports of mysterious telephone calls to the courthouse began to surface the morning after the trial's first day. First it was a female court attendant who got a telephone call. Then one of the court stenographers, another female, received an anonymous message. But when one of the female jurors became the victim of an obscene telephone call, Judge Huot laid down the law. The Sheriff's Department was directed to intensify security in the courthouse and particularly on the fourth floor, where the trial was being heard. The judge also ordered the jury to be sequestered for the duration of the trial. Donald Conway finally won one of his motions the hard way.

Judge Huot, a serious and busines-like jurist, had his difficulties with other nuisance-type matters at the start of what he knew would be a long and arduous proceeding. WABC TV, the flagship station of the American Broadcasting Company in New York, was petitioning the court to allow its camera crew inside the courtroom for the murder trial. The judge could readily see that the media wasn't going to relent or go away, but he denied WABC's lawyers the petition, sending them to the state Supreme Court on appeal. The other television stations continued to cover the trial, paying artists to sketch the defendant and the other players in this real-life drama.

"We don't need dramatics," declared Donald R. Conway, who at age forty-six was on a pedestal among trial lawyers in the state. Urbane and intelligent, Conway had gotten clients out of tighter predicaments than this. He was appalled by Prosecutor Calo's theatrics, or at least that was what he would have the jury believe. "You can't always assume that people in the courtroom are telling the truth," Conway continued in his opening statement. Lawyers, he said in a calm deliberate voice, "don't know what the truth is." The defense attorney admonished the jurors not to make up their minds before they heard him and the parade of witnesses in the exchange called cross examination. "Don't accept the witnesses' testimony before cross-examination. Believe me, things will change." It was a twenty-minute lecture, but when Conway finished, the ringing of the prosecutor's shouting damnation of the defendant still seemed to hover over the jury. A few of them looked awestruck by it all. One or two appeared frozen in a flinched position. But the reality behind Dennis Calo's shouts would set in soon enough, as the parade of 124 witnesses testified to the various facts and exhibits during the nearly month-long trial.

The basic credo that puts the American criminal justice system above and apart from most others in terms of quality and fairness is that often-maligned but fiercely protected standard of the courts: the defendant is innocent until proven guilty, at least in a court of law. Honest lawyers will concede that such a belief is merely a matter of form, true in only a small percentage of cases. Of course, a majority of citizens would likely insist that if a person were innocent, he or she would not be in court in the first place. But the best of the nation's trial lawyers would agree that even if a client is guilty, his legal counsel must do the best job possible to guard against a false conviction. Should the client admit to blame for, or even an accessory role in, a crime, a thorough defense attorney will fight to achieve acquittal. Such a legal battle must be waged, even if it means the guilty going unpunished. The advocate is interested only in the client's right to due process under the law. Likewise, if the defense wavers on a minor technicality, it is the prosecution's duty to try and claim the concession and use it to sway the jury, the people, to support all charges in the indictment.

Such was the dilemma confronting the defense team in the Cottingham case. Donald R. Conway, the senior defense attorney, and his associate Peter E. Doyne, had a client faced with charges that could add up to nearly two hundred years in a state penitentiary if he was convicted. That was the punishment Prosecutor Dennis Calo would seek if he convinced the jury that Richard Cottingham was the sadist who kidnapped and tortured five young women, one of whom was strangled to death. Conway and Doyne also had a client who fit that grey area defense lawyers must live with. Cottingham, who would testify in his own defense, had to be forthright to save the defense from the damage done by any embarassing surprises on the witness stand. To accomplish this, he had to admit to a strange fascination. Richard told his lawyers that since his youthful years he had had this fascination with bondage and the dark and mysterious world of sado-machochism, what the sex manuals call S&M. Normal sex—that is, good old missionary-style sexual intercourse—while satisfactory to most red-blooded heterosexual males—just did not provide the effect, the deeply needed sensual response, he needed. The administration of pain, that was different. The image and the helpless whimpering of a woman imprisoned in a slave collar, a mouth gag, and maybe a pair of handcuffs—these are the delights of those who might also frequent the coin-operated cinema machines inside many of New York's peep show parlors. This kind of activity might also be for those who passively like to watch and read about S&M.

But Cottingham was no spectator. True, he liked to go to places like the Continental Baths or Plato's Retreat, before New York's most famous center for topless and bottomless swinging moved out of the Ansonia Hotel to a new location at 10th Avenue and 34th Street. Once inside, one could watch couples of various preferences dancing in the nude, or get steamed up over the sights and sounds of partner swapping, or he might just brave it and join in the sexual bliss. And, yes, Cottingham was an avid reader. But he wasn't just willing to study the collection of S&M literature he kept locked up in his basement room, off limits to his wife and kids. His collection included such sensations as, "Harem Girls in Bondage," "Kidnapped by Bikers," and one of a series of books on the subject called "The Captive Bride." A quick look at the covers was explanation enough if you didn't have time to read. "Harem Girls," for instance, illustrated an "African Chieftan" with his woman on a short leash, attached to a slave collar, her pleading muffled by a leather gag. Conway and Doyne could visit their client's library during the pretrial period called discovery because the collection was in the hands of the prosecution, obtained by a search warrant executed that Thursday, in May 1980, when Cottingham was arrested. But the books, and the films, and the voyeurism at places like old Plato's Retreat were not enough for Richard Cottingham. He had to be with a woman, in the flesh. The cries had to be live, the fear convincing, or S&M just wouldn't be exhilarating.

It was an unusual combination, this defense team that would appear each morning in Courtroom 418, on the fourth floor of the majestic Bergen County Courthouse. Conway, the senior partner, appeared as the urbane, father figure, always outwardly confident. He was the seasoned counselor. The junior associate, Peter Doyne, was the image of the spanking new barrister straight from the classroom in "The Paper Chase." Doyne was young, clean cut, pinstripe-uniformed, bright, and boyish. Then, filling out the team, was the client, Richard Cottingham, highly intelligent and selfishly eager to play an active part in his own defense. A quiet and pensive man, Cottingham would often appear to be wearing a mocking smile. It was as if he knew the answers, only asking the question to see someone else on the spot and then answering it himself to appease a tremendous ego. He was always nervous, frequently twitching and fanning his legs like an accordion. He apeared studious, sitting between his two advocates. But he had trouble making eye contact. He was the type who would conduct a conversation, one-on-one, but turn his eyes downward or to the side. And always there was that icy grin he managed, even when the court guards escorted him back to his jail cell at the close of each court session. Seeing them sitting at the defense table together, somehow one got a distinct impression of the members of the defense team: it was an uncomfortable trio, one that just didn't seem right for each other.

It was not as if Don Conway needed the retainer when he took this murder-kidnap case. Since he had served as president of the New Jersey Bar Association in 1976, Conway's Hackensack law firm was abundant with clients and their money. He had never been the kind of trial lawyer to shy away from controversial or unpopular causes, however. Conway represented reputed organized crime people and small-time loansharks. Some of his clients were the twisted, even sinister type. When few other New Jersey lawyers were willing to take the risk of damaging their careers or images, it was Don Conway who willingly stepped forward to defend Robert Dilts. Dilts, a onetime influential Democrat, was forced to resign in 1971 as Bergen County Prosecutor after being charged in a State Police investigation with bribery, obstruction of justice, misconduct, and conspiracy. The state grand jury's indictment had strongly inferred that Dilts had been doing business with some of the state's more corrupt and unsavory characters—the mob. Dilts never returned to office, but his counselor succeeded in winning his acquittal, a feat the State Police would never forget, or forgive.

But if Don Conway, a dashing figure of a man with a handsome face and full head of impressive grey hair, was well known for his court conquests, so too did he live with defeats. Nor did he always appear as the courageous counselor, defending the honor of the decent sort of clientele who just happened to have the nasty fate of falling victim to an overzealous prosecutor or a runaway grand jury. It was no secret in the county's court circles that certain of his clients had caused Don Conway personal anguish. Not because his legal judgment might be tested or his ego deflated by a loss to conviction, but because Conway, like most family men, had to answer to a higher critic than his peers.

Don Conway lived with his wife, Virginia, in a beautiful, colonial home on a spacious piece of land in the upper-income community of Oradell in Bergen County. Not long after Conway agreed to take on the Cottingham case, reports circulated that he might drop out. The reports were dismissed by longtime colleagues as mere rumor, but there was something to the fact that some of Don Conway's cases had caused his wife and children, a family that was close and highly supportive of their proud husband and father, some pain. The Cottingham case, with its sordid suggestion of bizarre sex and the tawdry world of prostitution, brought back bad memories. In the early 1970's, Conway, twelve years out of law school and well established, represented Joselp K. McGowan, an elementary school teacher, in a murder case. It was a highly unpopular matter. The teacher was charged in the fiendish murder of a petite, seven-year-old girl, Joan D'Alesandro. Conway, who since received a firm reputation as a lawyer who refused to plea bargain with the prosecution, lost the case when McGowan pleaded guilty. And more recently, Conway defended another killer. The case remained fresh in the public's memory in Bergen County. Then there was the murder of a strikingly beautiful girl-next-door, Kimberly McIntosh. Her murderer, Lee Morgenstein, sentenced to fifteen-to-twenty years on a manslaughter conviction, was free after serving little more than five years in prison. The public was outraged by the murder and, in a new climate that clamours for the death penalty to be restored, the public was astonished and outraged anew with Morgenstein's release. Few would blame Don Conway. Most have forgotten that he represented the murderer. But the Cottingham case upset the sensibilities of his toughest critic in a household that brought two children up Roman Catholic. Yes, Don Conway had serious second thoughts about taking Anna Cottingham's retainer, but any vision of doom he may have forseen could not turn back the clock. Once an attorney begins a highly celebrated murder defense it is difficult, if not totally impossible, to exit gracefully.

As the widely publicized trial of alleged prostitute killer and woman torturer Richard Cottingham had caught the public's attention on those waning days of May 1981, the state of New Jersey was seeing a widening groundswell of feeling toward crime in general and murder in particular. And Bergen County, with one of the largest population centers in the state, was very much in the forefront of the new movement. Much of the sentiment stemmed from the treatment of convicted criminals. While the state, represented by Dennis Calo, the assistant county prosecutor, was trying its best to put Cottingham away, state law enforcement officials were fighting to keep other men already in prison from being released. One of those men was Lee Morgenstein, who, because Donald Conway had successfully won a twenty- to twenty-five-year sentence in the murder of Kimberly McIntosh, was soon to be paroled. Outrageous as it might seem, especially to those who could remember the 1975 murder as clearly as if it had happened the week before, the state's parole laws were heavily framed in favor of early release. The time was speeded for those convicts who were well behaved and unlikely to kill or break the law again.

The Morgenstein case was one of several examples cited by the growing number of citizens and civic and political leaders who favored the death penalty. The drive to return capital punishment was spurred by even more hotly debated cases, such as that of Thomas "Tommie the Rabbi" Trantino. Trantino had been convicted in 1964 of murdering two Lodi policemen. He was considered by correction officials as a prize example of the rehabilitated killer. But Bergen County, where the killings and the trial took place, was not ready for the parole of this devil from Brooklyn. The Trantino case became the cause cèlébre for the death penalty.

All the commotion over capital punishment, as the public clamoured about it into 1981, would be too late for Richard Cottingham's charge of homicide in the Valorie Street murder. But those who wanted to see Cottingham put to death could relish the fact that the defense had succeeded in separating the Maryann Carr murder charge from Cottingham's first trial in 1981. He would face that murder trial at a much later time.

## Eight

# The Victims

"Hey babe, why are you here?" asked the handsomely dressed man who had been sitting alone at the end of the bar. "Are you a working girl?" he continued. It was such a hackneyed approach, only someone as arrogant as Richard Cottingham could pull it off. In the case of Karen Corochi Schilt, the line worked.

Those were the first words he spoke to Karen as she was seated at a bar in a tavern on Third Avenue in Manhattan in 1978. Karen, a demure housewife from New Jersey, spoke in a faint voice as she testified in the beginning days of Cottingham's first trial. She was the leading lady among the four women who would testify to their nights of terror.

Karen was the perfect witness to introduce the subject to the jury. She didn't appear flashy in her purple and white blouse. Her dirty-blond, shoulder-length hair was neatly combed, falling tidily down around her horn-rim glasses. She was young, twenty-two, when it all happened two years ago. She had had two children and she was pregnant with her third.

Anyone with experience in reading a jury could readily see the potential empathy with this witness. There were several young female jurors. They undoubtedly would try to put themselves in Karen's place that cool March evening in 1978. There were also a few older women ... mothers who could sympathize with the witness's swollen, expectant condition. Then there were the men in the jury box, a number of whom had wives or daughters they would fight to protect from such an experience. Yes, Karen was the kind of credible-looking witness the prosecutor hoped for, the kind of woman who didn't get into a jam like this every day and one who certainly didn't look promiscuous.

Dennis Calo gently led Karen through her introduction, as a prosecutor should. She was working and living in New York City in March of 1978, waitressing at a restaurant called Tuesday's on Third Avenue near 17th Street. Karen's memory of events on March 22-23 was extremely clear for many reasons, she explained, but mainly because that was the time she almost got killed. As she told her story, the eighteen jurors listened intently and Richard Cottingham twitched his legs, staring down at some papers in front of him at the defense table.

Karen said she worked until about 6 p.m. on March 22, a Thursday, had one or two Pina Coladas and left Tuesday's at 6:30 to take a bus to First Avenue and 27th Street. That was the location of New York's Bellevue Hospital. The enormous public institution is a household name among New Yorkers because its psychiatric wing has held such notorious villians as David Berkowitz, the 44-Caliber Killer. But it also provides some excellent medical care to the more than 30,000 who are admitted there each year, and it was where Karen's husband, Henry, was mending from a broken leg. Karen visited for about one hour, cutting the time short because the mother of one of Henry's former girlfriends had been there trying to patch the old relationship together again. Karen and Henry were well on their way to divorce, but this premature boldness on the ex-girlfriend's part was more than Karen could take. She left Bellevue about 7:30 p.m. and headed back across town to the restaurant to play fill-in for another waitress who had asked the favor.

The hour went fast and Karen was still upset over her rather awkward experience with her husband. She was going to go straight home to her apartment on Third Avenue, but decided on the spur of the moment to calm herself with a drink. She stopped in front of a bar not far from her place of work and, taking an approving glance at the inside, walked in and sat down at a stool near the doorway. The place was slow, she noticed. Being a waitress herself, she counted the patrons. Three women, counting herself, a few businessmen sitting at the middle of the bar, and a man standing down at the other end, drinking by himself. She ordered a Seagram whiskey and Seven-up and sat quietly thinking about the fight with Henry and her pending divorce. She hardly had noticed that the lone man was no longer at the other end, but had moved over next to her. She sipped her drink as he began his warm-up.

"I told him I was a waitress and kept sipping my drink," Karen continued, telling her story from the witness stand. She had seen such persistence before in her restaurant job. Karen decided not to fight it. She would talk for a little and leave. She described him as in his early-to-middle thirties, about five feet ten and 170 pounds. A few of the more studious jurors broke their gaze on Karen to look over at the defendant as the witness continued to describe the man with light brown, almost blond hair. He was clean shaven and nicely dressed with a shirt open at the collar and handsome sports jacket. Karen could not recall his facial features, but she remembered the man's eyes. "He had beady looking eyes," she said.

She moved from the bar after some small talk and sat at a nearby table. She no sooner got comfortable when the man came over and sat down across from her. She told him she was getting a divorce, but planned to marry another man. After all, Karen told him, she was carrying her new boyfriend's child. A few minutes passed and the man went back to the bar, returning with two drinks. Karen recalled from the witness stand that she hadn't watched the man as he stood at the bar. He returned and she turned the questioning to him, asking if he was married. "He looked very upset," Karen said. "He clenched down on his lips and his eyes rolled, like he got really mad that I would ask a question like that."

As the man drained his second drink, Karen nursed her's. "I started feeling a little weezy, like I just had to lie down," she testified. "It was a funny feeling . . . like in the hospital when they give you ether." She felt that if she didn't leave that very moment, she would have to lay down right there in the bar. Karen thanked the man for the drink again, picked up her pocketbook and walked out onto Third Avenue. She walked, almost stumbled in the direction of her apartment, hardly off the same block as the bar, when a blue and silver-white car drove up close to the curb. The man inside rolled down the window on the passenger side and asked if she wanted a ride. "Normally I would refuse a ride, but this time I got in because I felt I needed one," Karen told the jury.

Karen next testified that she passed out in the car, gaining consciousness in time to see road signs for Interstate Route 80 in New Jersey. She recognized the area, she said, because she had once lived in Hackensack, which was about a ten-minute drive from the George Washington Bridge, connecting Manhattan and Bergen County in New Jersey. As she groggily watched the road signs go by, her sandy-haired kidnapper laughed and yelled out to her. "Hey Karen, do you know what this is?" She looked and saw he was holding a red and blue capsule. He asked if she wanted one, but Karen refused, telling him she didn't take drugs. He called it Tulenol. He shoved one down her throat, her tongue too limp to fight it, and she slipped back into unconsciousness.

When she opened her eyes again, Karen testified, the car was parked in a darkened area. She couldn't make out where they were. "Don't worry." he told her, "this is where I live." Karen had no way of knowing this at the time, but the darkened area was behind a brick apartment building known as the Terrace Apartments, a complex of apartments where Richard Cottingham lived with his wife and kids until 1975. Karen testified that she was too dazed to make out where she was or how long she had been there. And even if it had been light enough outside for her to see anything, there was a thick fog blanketing his car.

"I felt like I was dead," she told the jury. "I have the vague memory of being burnt on my breast. It really hurt, but I couldn't do anything about it," she continued. Then she had the sensation of being thrown from the car. "The next thing I recall is hitting the ground, feeling the ground underneath me and not being able to move or do anything." Karen said she was too weak even to yell for help. "It was like I was gonna die. I just remember wanting to go back home," she said. Her eyes opened and she looked at her body. "My arms and elbows were bruised and scratched up . . . my breasts were burned on the nipples. The burning sensation has stayed for two years," she testified.

Two physicians from Hackensack Hospital subsequently testified that Karen Schilt was examined in the hospital's emergency room on the morning of March 23. Dr. Harold H. Goldberg, a neurologist and psychiatrist, said Karen was in a comatose state when he examined her, explaining to the jury that a "combination of alcohol and barbituates caused her condition." Blood tests and analysis determined that Karen had been given Amobartital and Secobarbital, either of which, when combined with alcohol, are quite potent, the doctor said. Amobarbital and Secobarbital when combined in a capsule are known as Tulenol, but on the streets it is called a downer. Another physician who examined Karen testified that she was "dirty, semi-conscious, and occasionally moaning." Dr. H. Bruce Denson, an internist who serves as Bergen County Medical Examiner, said he found Karen's breasts had been traumatized, which is the medical way of saying her breasts and nipples had been bitten and burned. Dr. Denson made one other discovery. Karen Schilt's uterus was enlarged. She was as many as twelve weeks pregnant.

As Donald Conway rose from his chair to question Karen Schilt on the fifth day of the trial, he knew he would be attacking the first of the four most important witnesses in the state's case. As an experienced trial lawyer, Conway knew his technique must be sharp enough to destroy this witness's credibility. But his approach must also be cautious, because Karen had given a clear and coherent recollection of the events of March 22-23. She was a superb witness and one could read that the jury was impressed. And she had broken down in tears once, as she recalled "being thrown to the ground and not being able to move or yell for help." Conway must do something to reverse any feelings of sympathy the jury might have for Karen.

The defense attorney took Karen Schilt back over the same testimony she had given the morning before. He searched out any inconsistency he could find. One, quite a minor matter, dealt with the two Pina Coladas she said she drank at Tuesday's before going to see her husband at Bellevue Hospital. She now stated the time was six or 6:30 p.m., but in testimony she gave the previous week, before the jury was brought into the courtroom,* Karen had said she had the Pina Coladas at around 8:30 p.m. the night of March 22.

KAREN: "I guess I got my timing mixed up. I never testified before. I guess I was nervous."

CONWAY: "There was no jury in the courtroom last week was there?"

KAREN: "No,"

CONWAY: " You didn't break down and cry then, did you?"

KAREN: "I believe I did."

Conway attempted to establish that Karen Schilt, who had lived most of her life in the New Jersey communities of Carteret and Elizabeth, was unclear or shaky on her knowledge of New York City. For instance, Karen didn't seem to remember if Third Avenue was one-way going south, or one-way headed north. The Avenues

*Karen Schilt, as did each of the victims who testified, appeared at a hearing before the judge for the purpose of identifying the defendant. The jury was not present for these proceedings, which are known as *voir dire*.

in Manhattan go uptown, north, and downtown, south, and those like Third Avenue are one-way south. The lesson would not have much of an impression on people from out-of-town, but for New Yorkers, many of whom ride mass transit, it can be crucial. But even New Yorkers aren't very inclined or interested in visiting historical or famous monuments and buildings, like the United Nations. So when Conway ridiculed Karen for not knowing how to get to such sites, the point about her poor grasp of geography seemed to fall flat.

CONWAY: "Do you know where the Empire State Building is?"
KAREN: "Well, I've heard of it. I don't know exactly where it's located."

Conway brought out two points that Dennis Calo skipped, however. During Karen's testimony about the bar, she admitted that she said yes when Cottingham asked if she wanted a second drink, even though she had indicated earlier that she didn't particularly care to be talking to him and had moved from the bar to a table to be alone. Karen also admitted under cross-examination that the second Seagram's and Seven did not taste funny. If Tulenol had been added to it, she had not detected it in the taste. Karen also admitted that she had had a total of three and a half drinks. But as with his attack on her haziness about the time she had the Pina Coladas, Conway's hammering seemed to be blunted by Karen's answers and her determination to be truthful.

On another point, the defense attorney attached significance to Karen's description of Richard Cottingham. He questioned how she could have no clear recollection of his facial features. Again the witness astounded the defense by her response: "His face kind of changed because he gained weight and then lost weight," Karen testified, explaining that the defendant "was heavier in the lineup ... thinner now." And this observation couldn't have been more cogent, because Cottingham had lost about ten pounds from the time Karen viewed him in a police lineup on September 15, 1980, until Karen testified on May 25, 1981.

The crucial importance of a prosecution witness like Karen Schilt is her ability to identify her assailant in the courtroom, in the presence of the jury. The impact on the jurors can be devastating to the defense. It was, therefore, a shrewd maneuver on Donald Conway's part to try to disqualify Karen as a courtroom eyewitness—that is, her being allowed by the court to finger Richard Cottingham from the witness stand.

Detective William G. Thorne had first shown Karen Schilt sets of police photos, or suspect mug books, after questioning her about the 1978 attack. Karen insisted at that time that to make a positive identification she would have to see Richard Cottingham in the flesh. This was in June 1980, about a month after Cottingham was charged with the attempted murder of Leslie Ann O'Dell. A county grand jury was reviewing the evidence in the O'Dell matter, as well as several other crimes. Thorne, a detective for the county prosecutor's office, told Karen he would arrange to have the suspect appear in a lineup. Cottingham was subpoenaed to appear, but the lineup was not scheduled until September 15. During the interim weeks of the summer of 1980, Cottingham's attorneys were busy trying to block various investigative proceedings, including the requested lineup and efforts by New York authorities to obtain the defendant's handwriting samples.

At the lineup, held in a viewing room of the Bergen County Jail, Karen was introduced to Susan Geiger, one of the New York prostitutes who was kidnapped and assaulted. Susan, who had flown from Puerto Rico to identify Cottingham as her attacker, went into the viewing booth first. Susan unhesitatingly fingered Richard Cottingham as the man who attacked her on October 10, 1978. Karen was about to do the same when Peter Doyne and his associate, Paul Potenza, approached Sheriff's Officer Warren Chiodo to protest the lineup's going on without the presence of Cottingham's counsel. Dennis Calo, who was with Karen and Detective Thorne, had directed Officer Chiodo to bar Doyne from the proceeding. Calo and Doyne had a heated exchange, but Calo stubbornly refused to allow the two defense attorneys access to the viewing area.

Doyne immediately went to Judge Paul Huot's chambers to ask the judge to halt the lineup until his protest could be aired in a court hearing. Doyne wanted to see Karen's reactions, record her comments, and observe if there was any hesitancy before she made her identification of his client. These observations, including the length of time it might take for Karen to make up her mind, could become valuable if in the pretrial hearings the defense wanted to raise objections to the conduct of the lineup or attack the witness's certainty or uncertainty. Judge Huot listened to Doyne's protest and, as he later recounted, instructed one of his staff to telephone the jail and have the lineup temporarily halted for a hearing. Meanwhile, Karen was in the viewing booth watching as a half dozen men paraded onto a stage. Each of the men was instructed by Officer Chiodo to face front, turn sideways, and remove their eyeglasses. Karen watched until each had removed his glasses and motioned that she was ready to make a positive identification. Judge Huot's message arrived too late.

The United States Supreme Court, during the term of Chief Justice Earl Warren, set down a series of protections for defendants facing criminal trial. Among the requirements essential for a fair trial, said the Supreme Court (commonly known as the "Warren Court") was that the accused must have reasonable notice of the charges against him, an opportunity to be heard in his own defense, and, perhaps most important, the right to confront and question witnesses against him. In the New Jersey criminal courts there is what is known as the *voir dire* (French for "to speak the truth") hearing, when the accused has a full oppportunity to cross-examine the state's witnesses and present witnesses. The hearings are often referred to as Wade proceedings, for the Supreme Court decision in *United States v. Wade*. But in the Cottingham case, the hearing might more appropriately have been called a Stovall hearing, since it was the court's opinion in *Stovall v. Denno* that set standards for determining the basic fairness of out-of-court identification, such as in a police lineup. The Stovall decision is particularly important as a protection against the frequent use of methods of suggestion. To use an exaggeration, the police might put five clean-shaven men on a lineup with their suspect, who has three days of whisker growth on his face. The *voir dire,* hopefully for the defendant, would provide a determination of whether or not the identification was made under excessively suggestive circumstances. And furthermore, if the conditions were unduly suggestive, whether or not a courtroom identification would be irreparably tainted.

Don Conway set out to impress on Judge Huot that Karen Schilt had been shown two sets of police photographs—let's call them mug books—both of which included photographs of Richard Cottingham. With his picture in both books, one might reasonably speculate that if Karen had not made her mind up after examining the first set, perhaps she reached a more definite conclusion after seeing his photograph in the second set. Whatever his true motive, the defense attorney wanted to use the alleged method of suggestion to challenge Karen's competence. But as it turned out, he pressed hardest on the issue of defense counsel's being barred from the lineup.

"In *United States v. Wade,*" Conway declared at the *voir dire* hearing, "the Supreme Court said defense counsel can be present at critical times." Referring to the September 15 lineup proceeding, Conway continued, "At this point, the representation of Mr. Cottingham is critical." To this, Prosecutor Dennis Calo invoked a practical problem and a legal argument. Calo argued that the Wade decision may allow defense counsel to observe the lineup, but not actually participate. He pointed out that the viewing box, from which Karen Schilt, Detective Thorne, and himself observed the lineup through a glass enclosure, is a room of about twice the size of a telephone booth. It could not hold the witness, a detective, and two attorneys, Calo asserted with undisguised sarcasm. Furthermore, there were no charges yet filed against Cottingham with regard to Karen Schilt, Calo argued. Therefore, he concluded, Cottingham did not have the right to have an attorney present for

Maryann Carr. The twenty-six-year-old nurse was, as far as authorities know, Richard Cottingham's first murder victim. Her body, fully clothed except for shoes and stockings, was found outside the Quality Inn motel in Hasbrouck Heights, N.J., on December 15, 1977.

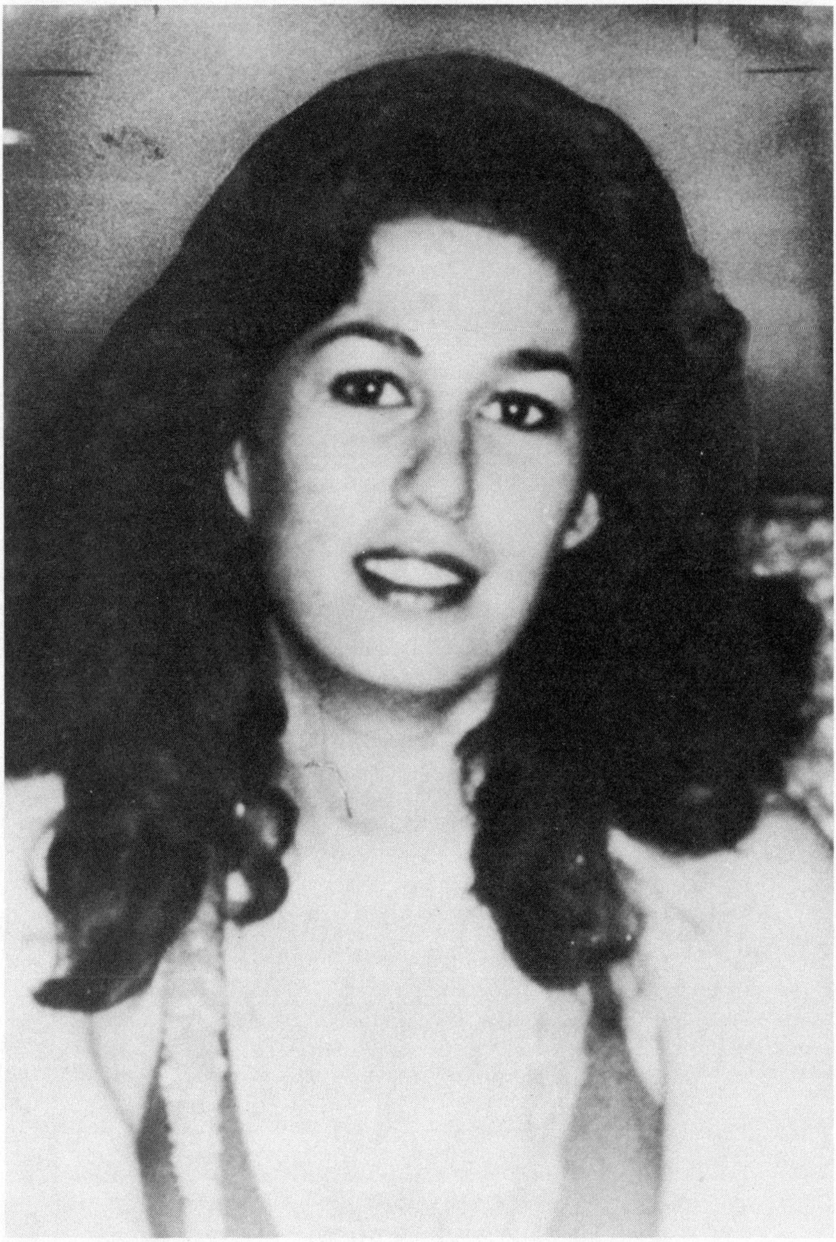

Deedeh Goodarzi. The identified victim of the Times Square Torso Murders, as they came to be called. (*New York Times* Pictures)

POLICE COMMISSIONER'S CIRCULAR No. 1
FEBRUARY. 1980

# POLICE DEPARTMENT
CITY OF NEW YORK

PLEASE POST IN A CONSPICUOUS PLACE

# WANTED

## INFORMATION REQUESTED HOMICIDE INVESTIGATION

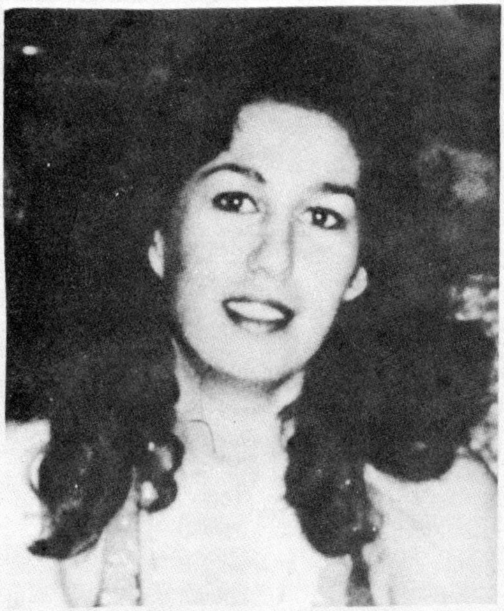

DEEDEH GOODARZI

Color of coat is black.

**Clothing worn by victim #2.**

THE ABOVE PHOTOGRAPH IS OF DEEDEH GOODARZI, ALSO KNOWN AS JACQUELINE THOMAS, JACKIE THOMAS, SABRINA, AND CRYSTAL ROBERTS. GOODARZI IS ONE OF TWO VICTIMS OF A DOUBLE HOMICIDE WHICH OCCURED DURING THE EARLY MORNING HOURS OF DECEMBER 2nd 1979, AT THE TRAVEL INN MOTOR HOTEL, 515 WEST 42nd STREET, MANHATTAN, N.Y., ROOM #417. BOTH VICTIMS HAD THEIR HEADS AND HANDS AMPUTATED. THE 10th PRECINCT DETECTIVE UNIT IS ENDEAVORING TO IDENTIFY THE SECOND FEMALE VICTIM WHOSE DESCRIPTION AND CLOTHING ARE AS FOLLOWS:

DESCRIPTION: **Female, White, 16-22 years of age, between 5′1″ to 5′4″ tall, weighing about 100 to 110 lbs. The clothing of this victim, pictured above, are, a black full length cloth coat, a pair of "bon jour" blue jeans, size 7/8, a pair of black patent leather boots, size 8 and a burgundy colored mohair sweater, size 38.**

PERSONS HAVING INFORMATION REGARDING THE SUBJECT OF THIS PHOTOGRAPH OR THE UNIDENTIFIED FEMALE, DESCRIBED ABOVE, SHOULD FORTHWITH NOTIFY THE 10th PRECINCT DETECTIVE UNIT, TELEPHONE 741-8245, 741-8225, 741-8229 OR 477-7448. CASE #1565/66, COMPLAINT Nos. 7615/27, DETECTIVE MICHAEL CLARK ASSIGNED.

ROBERT J. McGUIRE, Police Commissioner

Police flyer distributed during the extensive search for the Times Square Torso Murderer.

Richard Francis Cottingham. He was known as "Dick" to his classmates at Pascack Valley High School, where he graduated in 1964. His one extracurricular activity was running for the track team, but even in that pursuit he was a loner, never appearing for the team photograph.

Richard Cottingham. Even in a group or seated beside his attorney, he seemed to be alone. Richard listens pensively to Judge Fred Galda's remarks in a hearing to decide if a jury would hear the murder case involving Maryann Carr. Judge Galda listened to the testimony in the trial, Cottingham's second in Bergen County, giving New Jersey one of its first nonjury murder trials in recent memory.

Twenty-nine Vreeland Street, Lodi, N.J. Richard Cottingham and his wife, Janet, and their three children lived here from the mid-1970's until after his incarceration. The house contained a small metal safe, stored in Cottingham's "Trophy Room," containing a quarry of evidence, especially for the New York police.

Donald R. Conway. Handsome, self-assured, he was one of the most experienced trial lawyers money could buy. Near the end of Cottingham's first trial for murder and an assortment of assault charges, a newspaper reporter spotted Conway walking the wrong way toward a closed corridor. Told that his direction led to a dead end, the affable counselor turned and replied, "I'm beginning to catch on." He himself would face serious legal trouble about the same time his defendant was facing sentencing for the Valorie Ann Street case.

Anna Cottingham and Carol Jacobsen. Richard's mother and his oldest sister speak to reporters outside the county courthouse in Hackensack, N.J. Neither has ever accepted the state's indictment. Anna believes her son was the victim of a poor defense and Carol thinks a combination of forces beyond Richard's control joined together to frame her brother.

Richard Cottingham and Peter Doyne. Richard, dressed in prison issue clothing, is led to the court by sheriff's deputies. Peter Doyne, junior defense attorney, is beside the defendant with briefcase.

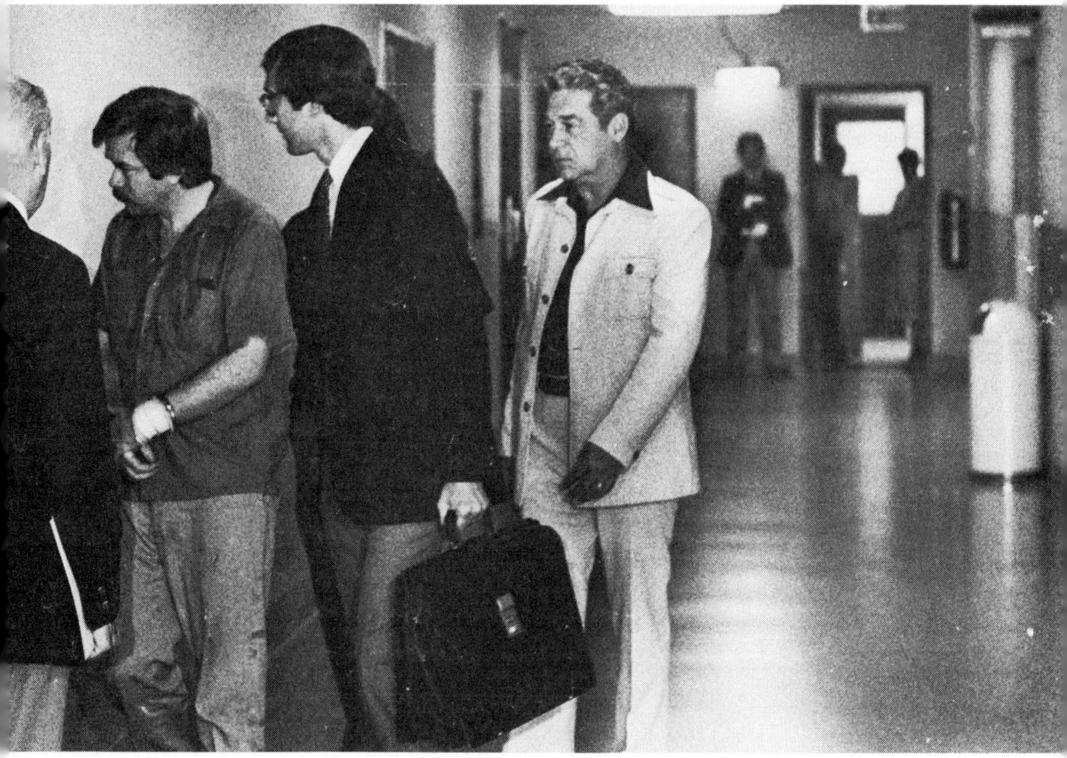

Richard Cottingham and Frank Wagner. Wagner, Bergen County's top public defender counsel, was Cottingham's second attorney. He pressed to have the second trial moved from Bergen County because of wide publicity from the first trial. Then he argued for the Maryann Carr trial to be heard by a judge instead of a jury. He won the latter argument, but the judge turned out to favor the prosecutor's case.

Paul R. Huot. Judge Huot's professional stubbornness nearly killed the state's case in the Maryann Carr murder charges. A hard-working, apolitical man, Judge Huot left little doubt of his personal feelings about the Carr case, but he disqualified himself from hearing the second trial.

Fred C. Galda. A former mayor, a former prosecutor, the workingman's judge, Judge Galda was criminal assignment judge in Bergen County and assigned the Maryann Carr case to himself. Then he decided to hear the evidence himself, rather than allow a change of venue or the selection of a jury from outside the county. He warned Cottingham that he was a former prosecutor, and the warning turned out to be more ominous than the defendant expected.

the lineup because it was part of the grand jury's investigative proceedings.

And so, with the jury out of the courtroom, it was up to Judge Huot to decide if Cottingham's rights had been denied at the lineup. Did he have the right to representation? This, it turned out, was stretching a technicality of the law. As the Rules Governing Criminal Practice in New Jersey clearly state, "while it is clear that the right to counsel obtains at a *post-indictment* lineup the extent to which it may obtain to *pre-indictment* identifications was not altogether clear following Wade. That question was resolved in *Kirby v. Illinois,* holding that the Wade-Gilbert rule does not apply to any *pre-prosecution* identification." Judge Huot ruled to allow Karen Schilt to identify Richard Cottingham in the presence of the jury. The judge said he found that "nothing occurred that can be considered unfair." Dismissing Conway's contention that the dual placement of Cottingham's photograph might be suggestive, Huot declared that "there were no verbal hints or clues." As for the confrontation between Doyne and Prosecutor Calo, Judge Huot was firm in his legal judgment, but also clear in his opinion of Dennis Calo's behavior. "It was rude, bordering on arrogant, to have gone on with the lineup over Doyne's objection," the judge declared. "However, the law does not punish rudeness."

"He's sitting between those two men right there," Karen Schilt sobbed, pointing to the defendant sitting between Conway and Doyne. "I'm sorry," Karen added, breaking down as she wiped the tears from her eyes with a white handkerchief. The prosecution would call her brave and forthright. The defense might sourly consider the performance theatric. But Karen's credibility was now with the judgment of the jury.

If Richard Cottingham ever had reason to hate women, he must have been furious as the prosecution witnesses took turns on the stand in Judge Huot's courtroom. All his women, including those who he had enslaved in his personal style of torture, were marching against him. Having their revenge, as it were, in some cases. In others, perhaps the testimony came involuntarily, but to the defendant the result was all the same—damnation.

Cottingham liked to date nurses. He had mentioned to some of his male co-workers at Blue Cross and Blue Sheild in New York that he believed nurses were among the most promiscuous females you could find. Perhaps it was because of the uniform or the fact that they were in a profession laregly reserved for women; whatever his reasons, the stilted view that nurses were all the same was one that Cottingham shared with a number of men. But Cottingham, married and the father of three children, went further than those less adventurous. He dated several nurses. Took them to discos and on occasion to a nearby motel where he could determine for himself if his beliefs were correct.

One nurse he dated was Jean Connolly, a single, twenty-eight-year-old who met Cottingham at the defendant's favorite bar in New York. That was in February 1980. Jean kept seeing Richard for several months. Long after that first meeting, February 9, Jean would clearly remember her social engagements with the sandy-haired fellow from New Jersey who operated computers. And the reason she could remember those dates so vividly, Cottingham would discover at his trial, was because Jean Connelly kept a careful dairy of all her social encounters. The personal calendar mentioned not only dates, but times and places. It was, as it turned out for the police, a perfect tool to track a man's alibi.

Much of Cottingham's alibi would be built around his employment record at the computer center in one of the country's largest group health insurance companies. Blue Cross and Blue Shield of Greater New York, known as the Blues in the health industry, employed two hundred people in the fourth-floor computer operation in its building on Manhattan's Third Avenue. The center operated twenty-four hours a day, seven days a week, offering operators, programmers, and supervisors a variety of shift hours and generous overtime benefits. Cottingham took advantage of both, working many weekends on the daily shift he preferred, usually 3:30 to 11 p.m. The schedule suited him because he could sleep late into the day, work his seven or eight hours, and still have enough leisure time to carouse at the bars or take one of his girlfriends to a disco. Or at least that was what he would have the jury believe he did with all his spare time.

Jean Connelly and another of Richard's girlfriends, Barbara Lucas, both nurses, testified on different dates during the trial, both recounting how they met Cottingham and telling the jury about some of the defendant's peculiarities. One observation the two women shared was Cottingham's use of an alias.

Like Jean, Barbara Lucas, a brunette who worked at Bellevue Hospital in New York, testified that she met Cottingham at Flanagan's, an Irish bar with live music that Cottingham frequented after work. But almost a year after they met, Barbara noticed that bartenders referred to Richard as "Jimmy." At Agly's, another tavern he took her to, Barbara asked him why the bartender called him Jimmy. "He said that sometimes he didn't give his real name in bars," Barbara testified. Jean recalled that Cottingham had introduced himself as "Jim" on the early morning that they met at Flanagan's, but she also told police that Richard would refer to himself as "Blair," the name of his oldest son. Defense attorney Don Conway elicited from Barbara that Cottingham preferred the name Blair because he didn't like his own name. But the thought the prosecution wanted to plant in the jurors' minds appeared undisturbed after Conway's cross-examination.

Prosecutor Calo led Jean Connelly through a review of her diary when the blond, pleasantly attractive nurse, who worked at Montefiore Hospital in the Bronx, was on the stand June 9, 1981. Jean's calendar showed a series of dates she had with Cottingham in March, April and May of 1980. A typical entry would say they met at the Blue Cross building at eight or 8:30 p.m. The dates indicated a variety of days of the week; March 11 was a Tuesday. The occasion of another date, April 12, was a Saturday, when they got together at about 6:30 p.m. Jean's diary would usually record that she was "out with Richard." Calo's motive was to establish that the defendant had a very flexible schedule at Blue Cross, affording him ample opportunity to come and go as he pleased. Don Conway knew what Calo was attempting, and he had to use anything he could find to destroy Jean Connelly's testimony by putting holes in the stories behind her diary. For example, Jean admitted under questioning that she began making additions to her diary after Cottingham was arrested in May 1980. She even acknowledged that she changed some of the entries and that she did this at the direction of police detectives. An example of one entry change was noted on April 18, 1980, when Jean recorded that she had a date with Cottingham. She admitted that she later wrote in on the date that the two went to the circus. It was an addition she made after speaking with the police, Conway brought out. But the sustained damage to the defendant might still be intact. After all, Jean had listed more than a half-dozen social outings when Cottingham had met her or picked her up in the evening hours when his work schedule would say he was supposed to be in the computer center at Blue Cross.

Barbara Lucas, who had dated Cottingham longer than any of the women he saw in his extramarital activities, seemed an unlikely candidate to want to hurt Richard. He had taken her on long weekend trips to the mountains or the New Jersey shore. They enjoyed each other's company at some of New York's more chic nightclubs and discos. Perhaps reluctantly, Barbara had told detectives of her former boyfriend's darker interests. When she was on the witness stand on May 30, Barbara was asked about a book entitled, *The Stalking Man*. A Dell paperback, the book was written by William J. Coughlin. "Richard had the book," she testified. "He said it was pretty good." Asked in the presence of the jury to explain the contents, Barbara said, "I read the book . . . it was about a guy who mutilated women, basically." Conway rose to object, but Calo persisted. "It's about a man who has a violent hatred for women . . . who preys on them in the streets," the prosecutor shouted. Calo insisted that the book be presented as evidence because it demonstrates "an interest by the defendant in this kind of activity." But as he had done with other pieces of sado-masochistic literature, Judge Huot refused to allow the evidence as an indication of Cottingham's state of mind.

One of Richard Cottingham's strongest alibi witnesses was a Blue Cross computer console operator who had been with the company in New York for twenty-three years. Anthony Forgione testified that he knew Cottingham, or "Cott" as the defendant was sometimes known at work, for thirteen years. Forgione testified to two very crucial dates in the indictment. The first was March 22, 1978, the day Karen Schilt said she was drugged, kidnapped, and tortured by the defendant. Co-defense counsel Peter Doyne showed Forgione a computer utilization log and a copy of attendance records from Blue Cross for March 22. The records showed Cottingham working 3:45 p.m. on March 22 to 12:15 a.m. the following day, which would include about an hour of overtime. Forgione told the jury that he recognized Cottingham's signature on the utilization log and the attendance sheet. He also testified that Cottingham had never signed for overtime he hadn't worked.

The next date Forgione testified to was May 4, 1980, the last day Valorie Street would spend alive in a motel room in Hasbrouck Heights, New Jersey. The attendance record showed that Cottingham worked that day, Forgione said, and the machine utilization log indicated that both he and Cottingham operated the computer for various jobs between 3:45 p.m. and the end of the shift on May 4. But May 4 was a Sunday, Prosecutor Calo pointed out, eliciting from Forgione that supervisors often were not as strict on weekends. But Forgione insisted that Cottingham, as far as he could recall, had never worked part of a shift, an hour or so, then absented himself from the center, and signed for the entire shift.

October 12, 1978, was another important date in the case against Richard Cottingham. Susan Geiger, a young prostitute, told detectives she was abducted and brutally beaten by a man with sandy-blond hair, blue eyes, and a clean-shaven face. But Arlene

L. Johnson, a seven-year employee at the Blue Cross computer center, testified that she had vivid memories of Cottingham being on the job October 13, the next day. And the reason those memories were so important, she continued under questioning from Peter Doyne, was that the defendant had a mustache. Ms. Johnson recalled the day, she said, because the pressure of the workload was so intense that she was instructed by a physician to relax in bed to recover from the trauma. "Richie was up there over the console every minute, doing this and doing that," she testified. "I remember that face . . . in my dreams that night the face had a mustache." Calo decided to leave this witness alone. He passed on the opportunity to cross-examine Ms. Johnson.

Not all of Cottingham's co-workers withstood cross-examination as well as Anthony Forgione or were left to leave the stand, like Arlene Johnson, however. Nor were all of the defendant's fellow workers quite as supportive. The defense found that calling these Blue Cross workers had its pitfalls. Cottingham's lawyers also learned that their client had his enemies among those co-workers in the computer center.

One of those fellow employees was not necessarily ambivalent, but the prosecutor was able to elicit a point from Eustice W. Griffith that proved seriously harmful. Griffith was called by the defense to explain the complexities of the computer operation at Blue Cross. The thirteen-year employee said he had been Cottingham's supervisor for two of those years and he described the defendant as an excellent computer operator, not only competent but reliable. The damage began, however, while co-defense counsel Doyne continued his questioning. Griffith acknowledged that he did not know if Cottingham worked on March 22, 1978, the date of the Schilt incident, nor did he ever sign approvals for payroll time. When Calo got up to question Griffith, he launched into this opportunity. Calo pulled out a date that had no relevance to the charges. It was May 7, 1980, two days after Valorie Street's body was discovered strangled at the Quality Inn. The computer utilization record showed that Richard Cottingham did not work that day, Calo began, but yet he signed for overtime. "Explain that Mr. Griffith," Calo shouted at the defense witness. Griffith, a middle-aged man who had meticulously explained the intricacies of computer science, glanced over the attendance record. "It appears to me," the witness calmly stated, "that Mr. Cottingham made an error and someone scratched it out in red."

Alan Mackey was a young man who worked as a subordinate to Cottingham for a period of about two or three years, including portions of 1978 and 1979. He was called by the prosecution to testify to another activity at the Blue Cross computer rooms. Speaking of Cottingham, Mackey stated that, "he'd come in five-to-six p.m. and disappear at times." These disapearances, Mackey continued, occurred on the weekend shifts. "Sometimes [it was] a matter of hours, sometimes I wouldn't see him again." Then the young computer operator let the jury know how these disappearances could go on without anyone being brought on the carpet. "The supervisor or the peripheral operators would cover for him," Mackey testified, adding, "I covered for him on occasion." Don Conway strained to reverse the damage by bringing out the facts that Mackey could not recall the dates of these "disappearances," nor could the defendant's co-worker tell the jurors where Cottingham went when he left the center. Other co-workers had testified that employees would leave for an hour or shorter periods to have a meal or move their cars to avoid parking summonses on the busy streets below.

Prosecutor Dennis Calo had some difficulty presenting two witnesses from among the group of Blue Cross employees who testified during the nineteen-day trial. They were questionable witnesses because of their motivation, and Judge Huot was rightfully concerned that the jury might misconstrue their comments. Bruce Huff and Dominick Volpe were being called to testify to certain discussions they had had with Cottingham concerning their mutual interests in prostitutes. Since no court officer can ever be sure what is going on in the minds of jurors, either when they are listening to testimony or, more important, when they leave the courtroom to deliberate, it is essential for a judge to instruct them on fine points of the law or on the implications of testimony that might be construed as speculative about the defendant's actions. Huff and Volpe were to testify to certain boasts by the defendant, Judge Huot stated. He warned the jury to consider only whether Richard Cottingham made the boasts, not whether they were true to his actions.

"Rich would brag to me about flashing large sums of money to these prostitutes," Bruce Huff testified. "He was able to talk them into paying them later on," the witness continued, meaning that Cottingham said he would promise to pay for a trick afterwards. Huff further stated that Cottingham discussed how he drugged drinks on one or two occasions and took the hookers to a motel in New Jersey. Defense attorney Conway was able to establish that the boast was made between Huff and Cottingham, with no third party to hear the conversation. But it was also brought out that Huff owed Cottingham $9,000. The reason for the debt was never disclosed, but it was revealed that Cottingham did a lot of gambling in New York and elsewhere. "You don't like Mr. Cottingham, do you?" Conway inquired in an icy tone. Huff responded with no hesitancy, "No, I do not."

Don Conway was only able to have Dominick Volpe concede that he and the defendant were not friends. And Volpe was equally as damaging in his testimony about these boasts as was Huff. "Most of the time we had any discussions it came up," Volpe said of Cottingham's boasts about hookers. "He told me he would meet them and show them a lot of cash and lure them to Jersey," Volpe related. Volpe pinpointed the periods of these discussions as covering 1978, 1979, and 1980. He said Cottingham spoke of picking up prostitutes on Times Square, one of the sleaziest centers of New York prostitution, and at the Hotel Americana, a more opulent location for higher-class prostitutes who work the tourist trade in mid-Manhattan. However, the most intriguing part of Volpe's testimony was when the prosecution witness explained to the jury a diagram of a nameless motel in New Jersey. Volpe said

Cottingham had drawn the diagram during one of their discussions about picking up prostitutes and luring them to New Jersey. The diagram showed the exits, entrances, and the parking areas of the motel. And, although Volpe did not identify the motel, the jurors had by that stage of the trial been taken through scale drawings and photographs of the Quality Inn Motel in Hasbrouck Heights, New Jersey. The jurors knew the motel was the final resting place for Valorie Street and they heard Leslie Ann O'Dell describe in lurid terms her captivity in Room 117 of the Quality Inn. Judge Huot had admonished them not to consider whether the defendant's boasts were true, but the diagram seemed to provide a strong antidote to his warning.

He had such an innocent face, Susan Geiger recalled of her first brief look at the sandy-haired man behind the wheel of the blue 1973 Ford Thunderbird. The first meeting was between ten and eleven the chilly fall night of October 10, 1978. Susan had just left a customer of hers, one of her regular weekly "dates," in his studio apartment at the Capitol Hotel, a shabby twenty-story building at the corner of 47th Street and Broadway. As she walked out onto the avenue, a man blew his horn and waved her over to his car. "He asked if I was a working girl, I told him I was, that I needed money," Susan recounted, sporadically fighting back tears as she testified on the eighth day of the Cottingham trial. "He pulled out a bunch of money he said he won gambling, like $5,000 maybe $10,000, or something like that, he said he'd won at dice or cards. He promised me $200 to go out for a drink and then some sex," she continued. But Susan, exhausted from her already full day and feeling the fatigue of her four months of pregnancy, told the man to call the next day. She gave him her number at the Alpine Hotel and headed home for the night.

Susan had been living at the Alpine with Eddie, her boyfriend and pimp, for three months. The Alpine is a filthy, run-down hotel that saw its better days when Eighth Avenue was part of Manhattan's bustling commercial district. But the better shops and restaurants had either closed or moved further east, to be with the moneyed class of customers. Susan was much the same way. She worked the more expensive hotels of midtown, like the Waldorf, New York Hilton, and the Plaza. "No. I would never work Eighth Avenue," she asserted, tearfully telling the male and female jurors of her career in prostitution. After all, Susan told them, "I charged $100 an hour."

A cute, if not particularly pretty blonde, Susan was introduced to prostitution when she was eighteen. She first came to New York in 1977 from Florida, where she lived most of her life with her mother in Orlando. She visited friends in Piermont, a suburban community in Rockland County, about twenty miles north of Manhattan. One of her friends, Joan Freyerson, had moved to the Bronx, where she ended up renting an apartment with Eddie. Tired of living in Florida and longing for the independence of being out of her mother's house, Susan decided to make one of her visits to New York permanent. She moved in with Joan and Eddie. The threesome lasted almost a year, when Eddie decided Susan would be better off if she moved closer to the action. Susan moved into the Alpine in July of 1978. Eddie, who by that time had become her boyfriend, lover, and father figure, lived with her most of the time. The relationship had been solidified. "I was a prostitute as long as I was with Eddie," Susan told the jury.

Dressed in a beige blazer, with a white blouse and blue skirt, Susan Geiger, twenty-two when she testified, had been living on her own in Puerto Rico for more than a year. But for all her suggested wordly appearance and independent means, she still cried like a child when she spoke of that night nearly three years before. She was a petite figure of a woman, skinnier now at ninety-seven pounds, her five-foot frame barely reaching up to the microphone in front of her at the witness box in Judge Huot's courtroom.

She testified that "Jim," the man with the Thunderbird, telephoned her at the Alpine the next day, October 11, 1978. They discussed the price and he agreed to pay in advance for a night of drinks and sex later at a hotel. "I told him I wouldn't go to any hotels except in midtown." They set a date to meet on Thursday night, October 12, at the Burger King restaurant next to her hotel. Susan walked into the fast food eatery at about midnight and looked for "Jim." She said she recognized him and described him again for the jury; sandy-blond hair, blue eyes, a mole near his mouth, about one hundred and seventy-five pounds. He was wearing wire-rim glasses, she recalled, and was dressed in a beige sports jacket, white shirt, and black slacks. He mentioned that he knew a nice place where they could go for drinks, suggesting they drive over to First Avenue in his car. "I told him I didn't go out in a car with anybody, but that I trusted him," Susan said, adding that she was satisfied when he told her he would give her the money once they got to his favorite tavern, Flanagan's, which is where he took his other girlfriends. She was a little concerned when they got to the bar, Susan explained, because she was unable to get a glimpse of the car's license plate. He parked the car so close to those in front and back that Susan couldn't make out the tag.

Flanagan's, one of Manhattan's popular meeting places for singles in the thirty to forty age bracket, was crowded as usual for that early morning hour, but Susan and her date managed to find a table. A country and western band provided the background music for the crowd, which that night was too busy talking sports or checking the availability of the opposite sex to notice the couple who had seated themselves not far from the band. Susan was more relaxed now. This was her kind of place, well insulated from the tackiness of the hotel bars and restaurants where conventioneers made it their business to paw and fawn over the women of her profession.

"He told me to go get him a pack of cigarettes, while he got us drinks," Susan said, continuing her testimony in the overcrowded courtroom. She explained that she hadn't been drinking alcohol or taking any drugs since she found out she was pregnant. But, she continued, "He said to please have a drink. I needed the money, so I said I'd have just one drink." When Susan returned with his cigarettes, "Jim" was seated at the table, busily stirring her drink, a vodka and orange juice. This seemed a little overhelpful, but she dismissed it. "He kept insisting that I drink it through the straw because the glasses have germs and you get high if you drink it through the straw," she testified. Over the drinks they talked about him and how he wanted a divorce from his wife. He told Susan he had five kids and lived in New Jersey. She stared into his face and watched his hand as he talked about his wife and his job in computers. "He was stirring it . . . he kept on stirring my drink for me."

Suddenly, she testified, "He reached over and grabbed my right breast real hard, very hard. I told him never to do that in a public place." "Jim" just smiled and told Susan her breasts were smaller than his wife's. Susan adjusting her body in the witness stand, blushed as she spoke of her anatomy. Cottingham's sister, Carol, sat in one of the front benches and eyed Susan Geiger intently, seemingly recording the witness's every word. The seat next to her was empty. Her mother, who had listened to Karen Schilt's tale of horror while attending every session of the first seven days, was absent from the courtroom the day of victim number two's testimony.

As her vodka and orange juice disappeared and the night wore into early morning, Susan Geiger began to feel drowsy. "He ascribed it to my pregnancy," she said, testifying that "Jim" sympathetically offered to take her back to the Alpine Hotel. He would pay her for the time and find another hooker for the rest of the night. But Susan didn't want to lose the earnings. "I told him the Remington [a hotel on 46th Street between Seventh and Sixth Avenues] was a very nice place to go." Taking her suggestion as an indication of her eagerness to make the money, "Jim" began probing just what he could expect from this hooker. "He asked me if I would do anal sex," she sheepishly told the jury. "I told him no," she continued, her voice growing stronger. "I told him there was no way I would do anything like that. I told him I would have normal, regular sex," Susan testified.

He suggested they leave Flanagan's for another place and he paid up the tab while Susan got herself ready. It was becoming difficult for her to fight the drowsiness; it was getting to her. As they walked to his car, she said, "He was practically carrying me." Susan was sinking into unconsciousness as they drove through New York that early morning. Her memory of time and space was vague. She remembered having maybe one or two drinks at the most. He might have had three or four. The time they departed from Flanagan's was probably around three in the morning of October 13. "I remember going over a bridge," Susan testified, trying to recall little things she noticed. "I couldn't even talk," she said of her weakened condition. "I remember looking up at the dashboard and trying to figure out what kind of a car it was," she said, recalling that the word "Thunderbird" was stamped on the dashboard. "He just sort of shoved my head back down."

A rustling of nervous anticipation seemed to come over the packed courtroom as Susan Geiger began recounting the next events. She told the jury that she recalled waking up and realizing she was in a motel room. He, "Jim," was all over her, "beating me with a hose or something and biting," Susan said in a choking voice. He was biting me "all over. I was trying to get him off me ... to stop hurting me because of my baby," she cried. "I scratched him ... but he was hurting me. He was biting me." Susan, the undivided attention of every juror and spectator visually locked on her dramatic display of emotion, stumbled over certain words as she described his sexual attacks. She was barely audible and had to be directed to speak up as she explained that he forced her to perform fellatio and brutally sodomized her until the pain and the drugs finally knocked her unconscious again.

"I felt drugged ... bad ... drugged, hurt, mentally and physically," she blurted in response to Dennis Calo's questions. It was morning and he was gone. "I woke up naked, bloody all over, on the motel room floor," she sobbed. "Bloody ... my nose, my mouth, my breast, my vagina ... all over," she said. "I tried to clean myself up," Susan continued, "I could hardly walk." She looked around the motel for her purse and her jewlery, but her belongings were gone.

She went out to the motel desk for help, "but the people were very cold. I told them to help me, that someone had hurt me." She told the person at the front desk that she didn't know where she was and that she needed medical attention. Someone, Susan couldn't remember if it was a motel worker or not, gave her a dime for the public telephone. Susan called her mother collect in Florida. Breaking down as she recounted the call, Susan said, "I told her [her mother] I had been beaten and raped and bruised all over . . . that I was very sorry for what I had done."

Captain John Agar was the first policeman to respond when the management of the Airport Hotel, a busy overnight spot surrounded by fast food restaurants and bars along Route 46 in South Hackensack, called about Susan Geiger. She was taken to nearby Hackensack Hospital and examined in the emergency room by Dr. Bruce Denson. Denson, the county medical examiner, could not testify about Susan's condition. He had just suffered a heart attack, but his written report was submitted to the court by Calo. A laboratory analysis showed that Susan's blood sample contained alcohol, mixed with Amobarbital and Secobarbitol, the same combination that had been found in Karen Schilt's blood the day after she was found lying in the woods in a Little Ferry apartment complex, not far from the Airport Hotel. It was Dr. Benson's report, sounding like a visit to a chamber of horrors, which confirmed Susan's torturous ordeal: laceration over the right eye, bruise on the forehead, bruises on the breasts, a bite mark on the right breast, bruises on the rectum and vagina, with severe tears to the rectal tissue.

Susan Geiger checked out of Hackensack Hospital October 13. There wasn't much more the hospital could do for her. She was patched up on the outside, given some medication for the discomfort caused by the lacerations and tissue bruises, but whatever injuries she had on the inside would have to heal with time. She had called Eddie, her boyfriend and pimp, and asked him to bring her some clothes, since the ones she was wearing the night before were disheveled and filthy. She was black and blue and still hurting from the swelling in her breast. But after she left the hospital, Susan agreed to go with Detective William Thorne of the county prosecutor's office and Detective Agar to police headquarters in Hackensack. She studied what seemed to her an endless procession of suspect photographs, citing only one as vaguely similar to her attacker because of the eyeglasses and similar hair color.

Before that Friday night was over, she and the two detectives had gone back to Flanagan's, trying to retrace her trail, and walked up and down Seventh Avenue in a fruitless search for her assailant. The only thing that proved helpful at all in the reports that Thorne and his partner filed for future use was the fact that Susan recognized the bartender at Flanagan's. Arthur Nicholson did not remember Susan Geiger, but he recalled that he saw "Jim," or Richard Cottingham, in the bar the night of October 12. Nicholson told the detectives he talked to the suspect about sports betting. "I just won some money," testified Nicholson, who also recalled that the man the bartenders sometimes called Blair left a three-dollar tip that night.

It wouldn't have been surprising if the then nineteen-year-old hooker had a few nightmares that night and a running number of nights after her ordeal at the Airport Hotel. But what happened that first Sunday night she was back in New York would be enough to unnerve anyone, even a street-wise prostitute like Susan who'd been around the block enough times to accept life's strange reality. Susan decided she was strong enough to venture out of her room at the Alpine for some Japanese style food at Kontiki's, one of her favorite oriental restaurants, located at the Americana Hotel. She had been through the lobby of the Americana hundreds of times, on her way to and from her customers. It didn't surprise her to see one of her "dates," but she was shocked when she saw "that man . . . the one who hurt me." The nameless, sandy-haired man with the innocent face was walking out of the hotel as Susan was headed for Kontiki's. "He asked me what happened to me that night," she testified. "I asked him why?" Susan panicked and started screaming, feeling threatened as the man stepped closer. Two men standing nearby in the hotel lobby approached to intercede, and he fled into the bustling crowd, disappearing from her life.

Three years later and nearly 1,400 miles from New York, Susan Geiger had settled into a new life in Puerto Rico. She was registered at the La Cancha Hotel in San Juan in June 1980 when Detective William Thorne caught up with her. Susan had ditched Eddie, left New York and returned to Orlando to live with her mother while the baby was born. She was by then twenty, still craving her freedom, too young to settle in with the child of a man whose love was as temporary as the pleasure it gave him when the baby was conceived and the pain she bore when their son was delivered. Susan had had a taste of the good life, and the $100-an-hour tricks had given her enough money to buy into a better lifestyle, even after Eddie had taken his share. Now in Puerto Rico, the money she earned working on her back would be all hers. She admited she lied to Thorne when he first questioned her after the incident. But Thorne knew all about her profession. He had been able to find her through a contact in the pimp squad in New York.

Detective Thorne brought along a folder of photographs to show Susan during the interview, and she again studied the pictures as intently as she had the night after her torture. In one file, he was number three, and in a second file, the face of her attacker bore the same resemblance to photograph number two, she told Thorne. "That's the man that hurt me," she said, "that's the one who did those things to me . . . . that tried to kill me." She agreed to return to New Jersey that summer of 1980 to see if she could help further with the investigation.

A county grand jury was sitting by then, receiving evidence for an indictment on the attacks against her and the other women. When she met with Thorne again, the detective took Susan to a field next to a body shop in Carlstadt, near Hackensack in Bergen

County. The field was covered with abondoned vehicles, cars and trucks that had been used in crimes. "Before he had a chance to say anything," Susan later testified, "out of about thirty cars, I picked the car. It [the blue Thunderbird] was dirty and the grass had grown up over it, but I recognized the car." Susan Gieger returned to Hackensack once more in September before Richard Cottingham was indicted for brutalizing her. On September 15, 1980, she met Karen Schilt, fellow victim and witness, and the two identified Cottingham in the police lineup.

Donald Conway had been studying Susan Geiger closely during her testimony on that eighth day of the trial. She was the quintessential prosecution witness: clear on her identification of his client, extraordinarily able to recall details, and just dramatic enough to convince the jury of her anguish and pain over an attack she surely had not imagined. But Conway had to destroy her credibility and he decided to use Susan's weaknesses as his weapon. Beginning his cross-examination, the defense attorney asked Susan to recall events just after the October 12 attack, when she was back at the Americana Hotel, a place where she had worked as a hooker.

CONWAY: "Weren't you back hustling at the Americana Hotel?"
SUSAN: "The way I looked. The bruisses I had. There was no way I could work."
CONWAY: "Were you arrested on October 16, 1978, for prostitution under the name of Mary Knopt?"
SUSAN: "Yes, but it was a mistake."

Judge Huot angrily cut into the cross-examination, barring the question and excusing the jury. "The arrest proves nothing," the judge barked at Conway. "If you have a conviction, that's something else," Huot told the attorney. But Conway protested. "She's a professional hooker who was not forced, as she says," Conway retorted. "She's putting on nothing but an act for this jury. She knows how to con people, how to con the police and how to con this jury. That's her motive in this case," the lawyer shouted. But Judge

Huot dismissed the argument. He had observed the witness during the moments when she sobbed and was overcome by tears when answering the prosecutor's questions. The judge watched her as Conway lashed at her; at one point when Conway was particularly aggressive, Susan begged the attorney not to yell at her. "It is the court's view that the emotional upset is not feigned," Judge Huot told Conway. "It is genuine." Furthermore, the judge warned Conway against using arrest or rap sheets to establish convictions, explaining to him, as if he were a novice barrister, that he "must have a certified copy of a judgment of conviction." And, finishing his admonition, the judge looked straight at Conway, the former state Bar Association president, and icily concluded: "Mr. Conway, you've been practicing law long enough to know what is proper and improper.

Conway attempted to further damage Susan's believability. He pointed out, and she conceded, that she had lied to the police about her profession. He impressed on the jury that Susan had returned to New York and her pimp just after the attack. She tried to explain that she loved Eddie, that her pimp was also the father of her child. But Conway again cut into her weakness, noting that she did not stay with Eddie long. "You loved him, yet you left him." But the cross-examination had missed its mark. It had sting, but it wasn't at all clear that the jury was so unsympathetic to this now twenty-two-year-old woman that it would not feel sorry to see her once again maligned by the defense attorney. It was not clear either whether Conway had done anything to remove that singularly solid moment of her testimony when Susan Geiger stood up in the witness stand, gazed out into the courtroom and, raising a trembling finger to the defendant, stated, "He was the guy that beat me, hurt me, that messed up my life."

If there was little humor in Judge Huot's drab courtroom, where the Cottingham trial marched relentlessly on, regardless of holidays or illnesses, it could be strongly attributed to the straightforward, business-like manner of the judge. Paul Robert Huot, who would turn fifty-five before he was finished with these proceedings, had been on the bench fifteen years, two of them as a Superior Court judge. New to the criminal field, he nevertheless succeeded in concealing his biases to the prosecutor and the defense. He owned the reputation of being tough-minded and fair.

The pressure on the judge in a highly publicized trial can be severe. Judge Huot was ultimately responsible for the behavior and whims of eighteen jurors, who included six alternates, or the substitute jurors who may or may not be needed to dispose of the charges. The nine men and nine women were being housed and fed in almost total isolation from family and friends—sequestration allows only restricted contact with loved ones—during their stay at a nearby Ramada Inn. The emotional strain can be devastating, and the judge must see to it that a physician is on call at all hours to see to any discomfort, be it physical or emotional.

The Bergen County Sheriff, Joseph Job, estimated that the trial was costing his department as much as $3,750 a day to pay for the jury's needs and compensate his staff of security guards and deputies. This estimate would not include the direct costs of the court and the prosecutor's office. But it was safe to estimate that the final bill the taxpayers would be handed for this trial would mount to more than $100,000. But in spite of all the expense for resources and manpower, there was an ironic note. Don Conway complained on the fourth day of the trial that his client's meals, served to him after he was escorted in chains and under heavy guard from the courtroom each noon hour, were ice cold. Even these simple matters received the attention of Judge Huot, who ordered that Cottingham be served a decent lunch. Huot wanted no unnecessary problems, no interruptions, and, most important of all, the judge wanted to leave no reason for the defense to call a mistrial.

If Judge Huot had set his mind on Cottingham's guilt or innocence, only the slightest indication came on June 6, the seventeenth day of the trial. The incident also provided the only occasion for levity, even if it was the darkest of humor.

The defense was prepared to present a Harvard University professor to testify about his studies of sado-masochism and bondage. Dr. Park Elliot Dietz, a psychiatrist and member of the teaching staff at Harvard Medical School, would testify that his studies found that thousands of people in the New York metropolitan area participated in and enjoyed S&M and bondage. If permitted to take the stand, the psychiatrist would observe that handcuffs and adhesive tape were stock tools or standard equipment to this fad or cult of sexual deviance, as some might see it. With the jury out of the courtroom, Dennis Calo protested the introduction of Dr. Dietz's studies. The young prosecutor called the psychiatrist's findings irrelevant to the case. The doctor had not been in any of the motel rooms to observe Richard Cottingham and his victims, Calo argued, terming the testimony "pure, unadulterated speculation." But Peter Doyne, the assistant defense attorney, countered that the jury might be under the misconception that S&M and sexual bondage are rare. "I think they [the jurors] are entitled to know that bondage and sexual sadism is not confined to Mr. Cottingham," Doyne argued. Once again, Judge Huot's uncanny insistence on common sense blocked the defense's argument. "If it's as widespread as you claim Mr. Doyne," Huot said, "how do you know they [the jurors] don't have knowledge of it?" The psychiatrist has no personal knowledge of this case, the judge continued, and his testimony would be purely speculative. "I see no need for the jury to be entertained by an erudite psychiatrist's study of the habits of a portion of the population," Huot said in barring the testimony. But the judge's next observation was far more telling of his own beliefs. In dealing with the evidence and testimony, Judge Huot stated, "the proof of the Street murder hinges not on the use of handcuffs and tape, but on the fingerprint."

Prosecutor Calo had promised the jury in his opening remarks that Valorie Street, the "silent victim," would "speak" before his case against Cottingham was completed. "Richard Cottingham left one thing in that room," Calo had said of the motel room where the young prostitute's body was found. "That was his identity itself . . . his fingerprint found on the handcuffs, lifted and preserved." And Valorie Street did "speak" at the trial, not only through the experts who examined the handcuffs, but through people who had known her and saw her, even after her death.

Just nineteen when she was strangled, Valorie had started out in prostitution at an early age. Before she was encouraged by a pimp to come to New York in 1980, she had worked the trade in Florida, ending up at a place called Fantasia Health Spa, outside Miami. Vickie Lynn Street, Valorie's younger sister, said the two girls lived with their father in a town called Leisure City, while Valorie was turning tricks at the health spa. The two sisters frequently quarreled before Valorie decided to leave in March. Valorie worked the streets of Miami for a short time before she was arrested and put in the lock-up for a week. That was in April. Theresa Gribble, another nineteen-year-old hooker, said she first met Valorie in New York City in early May. They shared a rooom at the Hotel Seville, the same hotel where Jean Reyner was stabbed and mutilated on May 15, 1980. Theresa also said she and Valorie shared the same pimp, whose name, ironically enough, was Lucky.

Theresa Gribble's testimony was important to the prosecution because she was one of the last persons to see Valorie alive. Theresa recounted how she and Valorie went out shopping on May 3, a Saturday. Later that night, Valorie went out to work without her. The time was around nine o'clock, when Manhattan's night life is just getting started. She remembered seeing Valorie at the corner of Madison Avenue and 32nd Street, a popular working place for hookers. Valorie was dressed in a white, short-sleeve T-shirt, baby-blue jeans, and biege tennis shoes. Theresa recalled, among other things, that she had dyed Valorie's hair strawberry-blond and that the two talked about home and how they sometimes missed their families. She could not recall if Valorie was wearing jewelry that night, although detectives would later find that Valorie's pierced earlobes had only a single, gold, heart-shaped earring in the left ear. "She said she was going to meet a trick," Theresa testified, "a guy who pays you for whatever." And as for Valorie's last words to her final friend, they seemed classic of this sidewalk world of flesh sales and peep shows. "I believe she asked me for some rubbers,"

Theresa said, explaining that she gave her girlfriend a package of protection before Valorie disappeared into the night to perform her last trick.

Theresa Gribble was decidedly unhappy and uncomfortable with her role as a witness. She had moved back to Ohio with her folks when she was called, or, rather, subpoenaed, to testify. She was held as a material witness throughout the trial, confined in special "jail" quarters that once served as the sheriff's residence. Lucky, the pimp, could not be reached to testify. He was last reported hiding in Philadelphia, a thick folder of arrest warrants keeping him from returning to New York. It was believed that Valorie had spoken to her pimp just before she disappeared. There was also a report of her being seen entering a blue, two-door Cadillac with a New Jersey license plate, but Theresa Gribble's testimony indicated that this had been earlier in the evening.

Donald Conway didn't allow Theresa to leave the witness stand before eliciting some valuable information about the risks of being a prostitute. The nineteen-year-old hooker, or ex-hooker by then, was exceedingly nervous, bordering on hostile. Dressed in a bright, plaid flanel shirt and dark slacks, she stared coolly at the defense attorney, insisting on replying in one-sylable words to his prying questions. Nevertheless, Conway was determined to establish that a prostitute's life was not devoid of violence, even if Valorie's fate was one of rare circumstances.

CONWAY: "Had you ever been beaten by a trick?"
THERESA: "Yes."
CONWAY: "Is that a fairly common thing?"
THERESA: "Yes."
CONWAY: "Had you ever been beaten by the pimps?"
THERESA: "Yes."

Theresa Gribble, who had worked as a prostitute for about three years, also acknowledged the high drug use among hookers. Conway also wanted to know how frequently hookers encountered customers who insisted on using handcuffs and violence to enliven their sex. "This is a practice engaged in by some people who like women for that purpose..." Conway started, but Judge Huot cut him off. Conway was also trying to establish that the threats of violence are sometimes only subterfuge, not always followed through. "Threats without the intent to harm are irrelevant," Judge Huot interjected, "because each of the witnesses was in fact harmed." The judge lectured Conway, saying that that kind of testimony could be obtained from any number of hookers. "You and Mr. Doyne could go to Madison Avenue and 32nd Street tonight and find someone who could tell you that," the judge said.

The staff at the Quality Inn saw very little of Valorie Street during her stay there on the weekend of May 4-5. One person who saw her for any length of time was a maid named Mary Sansanell. Mary was working on the morning of May 5. There had been some talk that the Sunday maid had had trouble getting into room 132. She had tried it at about 9:30 Sunday morning, but the door was double locked. When she had come back a half-hour before noon, she entered the room to find that the second bed was stripped down to the mattress cover. The cover was soaking wet, the Sunday maid said. But when Mary Sansanell made her rounds that Monday morning at about 8:40, both beds appeared unused. "The second bed was neat," she noted, "but the bedspread was pulled down tight on the front, like you want to hide something." Mary began to vacuum the room, working her way over to the second bed, near the window. She pushed, but she couldn't get the sweeper under the bed. "So I picked up the spread," she testified. "I saw an arm ... [and] I went out and screamed." Authorities arrived shortly after Mary's screams beckoned help. But it was too late for Valorie Street, whose body, nude but for a pair of cheap Hong Kong handcuffs around her wrists, was found jammed under that second bed.

If Valorie could have testified about her own murder, she probably would have done so in the strongest terms. Certainly she would have mentioned her imprisonment in those handcuffs. But since her voice was stilled, another spoke for her. He was an expert from the Washington headquarters of the Federal Bureau of Investigation. William J. Van Atta would be the voice of Valorie's cry for vengence.

Van Atta had received and examined two separate series of prints related to the Cottingham case. One series was sent to the FBI's Washington-based laboratory on May 14, nine days after Valorie's body was discovered. Another series was hand-delivered on June 5, 1980, not long after the attack on Leslie Ann O'Dell. And here was the nub of some confusion to come. There was little doubt that the jury might safely assume that the series received by Van Atta on May 14 was the sum total of prints pertaining to the Street murder. Likewise, if they were not specifically told different, the jurors might think that the June 5 delivery to Van Atta was the sum total on the O'Dell incident. If there was any natural inclination for the jury to draw these conclusions, than the defense would certainly want to exploit the confusion. The questions that might be on the minds of the jurors was this: if the Bergen County Prosecutor's office had found latent prints from the handcuffs on Valorie Street on May 5, why wouldn't those prints be in the series sent to Van Atta on May 14? But this wasn't the case. For one thing, someone had misplaced the record of the latent print. For another, on May 14, eight days before Richard Cottingham was arrested after leaving Leslie O'Dell, the authorities did not even know of Cottingham as a suspect, much less have his prints to compare with the thumb print found on the Street handcuffs.

The prosecutor, through design or incompetence, never succeeded in clarifying why it was not until June 5 that the latent thumb print was received by Van Atta. It took the common sense approach of Judge Huot to clear the confusion. But Conway took a stab at reaping some benefit from the situation. After all, the fingerprint was the most powerfully convincing piece of evidence the prosecutor would present. When Conway asked Van Atta, who answered questions in a straightforward and forthright manner, the results of his examination of the May 14 prints, the FBI expert was compelled to say that all but the fingerprints of the victim were of no value.

But before Van Atta took the stand to answer Conway's questions, Judge Huot had Calo and Conway approach the bench and agree to tell the jury just what the FBI fingerprint analyst examined on those two dates. On May 14, the FBI laboratory received Valorie Street's prints, along with those lifted from a box of matches, the "do Not Disturb" sign, and the showerhead in room 132. And on June 5, Van Atta received a series of prints that included those lifted from room 117 after the O'Dell attack, and the latent print taken from the Street handcuffs. So it became clear to the jury that when Van Atta testified that he found no value to the prints taken from room 132 and delivered to him in the May 14 series, he was not talking about the state's most important evidence.

Van Atta was the final witness in the prosecution's case. It became his turn to testify just before lunch on June 5. He was most undramatic in his delivery and it became obvious to Calo that this final punch had missed the target. So the prosecutor, who had learned new tricks by this stage of the trial, broke off the questioning at the adjournment, indicating he would continue with the FBI specialist after the recess. When he returned to the stand, Van Atta remained standing, positioned in front of a display of photo enlargements. He pointed to the thumb print, blown up eighteen times magnification. It was true, he said, he had no knowledge of where, when, or under what circumstances this thumb print was lifted. However, on the basis of his study of the defendant's fingerprints and the thumb print taken from the handcuffs, Van Atta asserted, "It is my conclusive opinion that these were made by one and the same individual."

*Nine*

# The Defendant Speaks

Only Richard Cottingham could reveal what was going through his mind that sixteenth day of his trial, June 6, 1981. The defense was taking its turn before the jury. The stocky defendant rose to his feet at the defense table, situated on the far left of the judge. He began a slow, seemingly awkward walk toward the jury, to the witness stand at the judge's right. There was the chill of an electric shock in the courtroom as the reality sunk in. The man accused of nineteen brutal crimes against five different women, all of whom had testifed in one form or another, was finally having his day in court.

Dressed in a conservative grey suit, his mustache nearly concealing his tight upper lip, Richard Cottingham looked nervous. He was the first witness called by Donald Conway. But, as it was later learned from one of his attorneys, this was Richard's idea. He wanted to testify.

One could almost dismiss, for the moment, all that had been said against him. Watching Cottingham, one could almost share his humiliation and embarrassment. Here was a man, the father of three young children, who had spent many of his adult years working and providing for a family. But the jury was not seated to hear about this man's children, his wife, or his sense of pride and responsibility. It was the dark passage of Richard's life the jury wanted to know more about. He was coming forward to speak in his own defense, not to provide a resumé of his domestic accomplishments. Would he defend the lifestyle he apparently enjoyed in secret from his family? Would he be able to speak of this with his mother and sister sitting in the same front row seats they had occupied virtually since this nightmare of charges began to unfold? It was almost as if he realized he'd made a tragic mistake, this—his—decision to testify in his own defense. But it was too late to turn back now. He shifted his muscular body toward the witness stand, stumbling nervously as he realized he had entered the seat from the wrong side. All eyes were fastened on him as he tried valiantly to cover for his clumsiness. His voice was almost inaudible as he took the oath to tell the truth.

Silence fell on the courtroom as he began his testimony, prompted each step of the way by the steady voice of the defense attorney. He recited his school experience, his employment record, and the details of his marriage to Janet in 1970 and the children he had fathered. He explained how his marriage had started the gradual decline toward divorce. His manner could barely disguise the edginess, even under the amiable conditions of having his own attorney take him over obviously rehearsed background. Still he fumbled awkwardly on the most minor of points, answering yes to a question of whether he had worked a particular day, and quickly correcting himself by explaining he could not have been at work May 21, 1980, the day before his arrest, because he was in divorce court. He was challenging the divorce, he said, because his wife was demanding that she be permitted to take the children out-of-state. However, he did not contest the grounds for the divorce, the complaint of mental cruelty. This stemmed from the fact that he had rarely been at home during the last several years of their marriage. "She believed I had a girlfriend.... Yes, I did," he admitted.

This was all very educational, perhaps perfunctory, these gratuitous details of his and Janet Cottingham's domestic affairs. But it was just the warm-up. Even if the jury had anticipated they would hear Richard Cottingham testify, it is a safe if only an educated guess that the jurors did not expect to hear such a candid acknowledgement of this man's sexual experiences away from home. That was just the start, however. His admitted experience with bondage was something else. But while he vigorously protested his innocence to the charge of murdering Valorie Street and denied even knowing Karen Schilt, Susan Geiger, and Pamela Weisenfeld, much less attacking them, Cottingham did not deny he was arrested after leaving Leslie Ann O'Dell. And the jury had heard Leslie, tearfully graphically, and persuasively chronicle the brutality of this defendant. They had listened intently to the horrors detailed by Karen Schilt and Susan Geiger. The victims had spoken and their act would be tough to follow.

"She said if the money's right, she'll do anything," Cottingham said, admitting to his bargaining with Leslie O'Dell. "I said if the money's right, we'll get to know each other and have a nice social evening. I found it easier to let *them* quote a price," the defendant explained, as if he might be describing his experience of negotiating the price of pottery on a street in Athens. And so it continued. What the jurors did not learn from the women who testified, they would hear from the defendant, as he unabashedly recounted his experiences. Hookers, he told the jury, were a flesh commodity that depended on color as much as anything else. Black prostitutes usually went for $10 to $15, white girls of the street could usually ask $15 to•$20, and the uptown hookers, the higher-class whores who worked out of the fancier hotels, these women could demand much more. His negotiations with Leslie continued, he explained, with Leslie first demanding $450, coming down to $250, and than settling for $180, if he could deduct the cost of food, alcohol, and whatever other expenses the night of May 21, 1980, might bring.

"I told her that for that kind of money, I was into a bondage-type situation. I told her I enjoyed seeing girls in bondage and that she would not be hurt. I explained to her it might involve tying her up, possibly spanking her with my hand. I told her it was more a thing of seeing her in leather," Cottingham told the jurors of the negotiation for his fantasy with Leslie. "The whole idea of bondage," he said, "had aroused me, or fascinated me since I was young . . . it was something a little different . . . out of the norm."

He assured Leslie, Cottingham told the jury, that he was not interested in inflicting pain. "I explained to her they are two different things, like night and day . . . people who are into bondage do not do S&M and people who are into S&M do not go through the theatrics of bondage. I told her for that kind of money I would want her to do almost anything I asked, but not including hurting her." It would mean any kind of sex, he continued, which could mean "orally, anally, in the bathtub, almost anything that came to mind. When she realized she wouldn't be hurt, she agreed."

His arrogance seemed boundless. The defendant had formed certain opinions of the jurors. He saw the potential in the female jurors. But he had some ideas about a few of the males as well. Cottingham had come to the conclusion that two of the jurors were gay, one of his lawyers said later. And so he told the jury he had bought the leather gags and the handcuffs found in his briefcase from a friend who was gay. He thought that detail might gain some sympathy. He had other strategy based on his perception of the jurors. He said he carried adhesive tape in the car because he had difficulty changing his son's paper diapers. He also looked for some parental empathy when he told the jury that the toy guns the police confiscated were purchased for his boys, Blair and Scott. And, to demonstrate that he had compassion for prostitutes, he acknowledged having drugs . . . that he purchased them in New

York for a friend who was a hooker. He provided her with the drugs so she wouldn't get busted, Cottingham told the jury.

Besides his "fascination" with seeing women in leather, the defendant also acknowledged one of his other life-long dreams. He wished to become an accomplished gambler. "I grew quite avid over gambling and quite good at it," Cottingham said in an almost boastful tone. His real successes came with liar's poker, he related, explaining why he carried a bundle of one-dollar bills, usually one hundred of them, with a twenty wraped around the outside. He modestly admitted his weekly winnings at poker was about $75 to $80, but that betting on sports events would bring in $500 to $800. Even with these supposedly modest earnings, the defendant's arrogance was barely concealed. "I was one of the few people I've ever known to gamble and come out on the plus side," he told the jury.

But for a man who claimed attentiveness to his children's most minor needs, like adhesive tape to keep the baby's Pampers from falling off, Cottingham must have seemed a true enigma to the jury. Sharp on details and dates, but casually forgetful and even vague on particularly critical points.

This was where Assistant Prosecutor Calo showed his strengths. His masterful grasp of the most minor of Cottingham's inconsistent or evasive answers made Calo's cross-examination brilliant. The defendant could exhibit startling recall when he wanted to, but when Calo asked why he told investigators the day of his arrest that he had never before been to the Quality Inn Motel—where he and his girlfriend had had several trysts—Cottingham said he did not remember the motel visits "at that point."

Do you recall biting Leslie's breast? Calo bellowed. "Not particularly ... no," the defendant responded, almost cavalierly. He recalled nothing about a laceration to the nineteen-year-old prostitute's breast, Cottingham said as he viewed a photograph of the victim. "All I see here is a scratch," he stated, scarcely concealing his sarcasm.

Why did he have one of the toy guns, supposedly meant for his children, when he was arrested? the prosecutor pressed. The defendant said that Janet, his wife, wouldn't let him give the gun to his kid. He had acknowledged a fascination since boyhood with elements of female bondage, but when asked, the defendant said he had only begun carrying the leather gags and handcuffs about the time in May 1980 when he met Leslie. He denied placing the gag on Leslie, however. "No," he replied, "it wouldn't have fit across her mouth."

In what might alone have served as a fatal blow to the defendant's self-perceived ingenuity, Calo returned to the defendant's claim that he kept rolls of adhesive tape for the children's diapers. Cottingham acknowledged he had an open roll of tape with him the day he was arrested leaving the Hasbrouck Heights motel. "You didn't have any Pampers on you at that time," Calo stated acidly. One could almost feel the scorn in the courtroom. One keen observer said he thought he saw a few of the jurors glancing skyward, quickly composing their faces after the smirk of contempt for the defendant.

"I am deeply embarrassed and ashamed for getting into these episodes," he told Judge Paul Huot before the judge had announced maximum sentece of 197 years. "If ever I get out, I will never do anything wrong or break any of society's laws again." A stern-faced Judge Huot was not impressed. Huot said he was deeply distressed with Cottingham's unwillingness or, more accurately, his "inability to realize that he did anything wrong." Judge Huot, a man of deep regard for the moral and legal codes that help keep some order in an otherwise senseless war among society's members, could hardly restrain his contempt for Cottingham, a man who viewed prostitutes as "objects to be used and abused." Characterizing him as highly intellectual but "totally amoral," Judge Huot looked to the safety of all women in the defendant's reach. "The sentence," he declared, "must be for the protection of modern society."

*Ten*

# Still Bitterly Disappointed

"That was our big thing with Conway. He wasn't prepared."

Carol Jacobsen was a bitter women. She watched her mother, Anna Cottingham, a 73-year-old widow trying desparately to help her son, sell her Florida home to pay the final bill from Donald Conway. It cost the family more than $35,000 for the defense, and what had they received? Richard Cottingham, Anna's only son, was given a jail sentence of 173 to 197 years for the murder of Valorie Street and the kidnapping, assault, and sexual torture of three other women. It was a bitter pill for Carol. She still insists that conway "sold out" her brother.

"My brother didn't murder anyone," she asserted. Although Carol concedes that Richard was "involved" with prostitution, gambling, and loansharking, she stubbornly argues that her brother is the real victim. She even suggested that, because Cottingham brushed with serious criminal activity in New York, the Mafia was "out to get him." She speculated that Richard made enemies with his gambling by using his winnings to freelance as a loan-maker. If it is true that he made loans and demanded high interest, or vigorish as the loan sharks call it, Cottingham would not have endeared himself to the underworld. But such small competition could be eliminated much easier and with greater swiftness than the slow, if deliberate, pace of the courts. Nevertheless, Carol Jacobsen believes someone did her brother in. If it wasn't organized crime and Cottingham's flirtation with their ire, than it was the people who run the criminal justice system. And her mother, if no one else, agrees. "It's the biggest farce I've ever seen," Anna Cottingham tearfully declared on June 11, 1981, the day her son was convicted.

Carol Jacobsen speaks with a soft voice, gently laced by a slight drawl acquired in the half dozen years of living in southern Florida. She can be very intense on serious subjects, such as the fairness of justice, but she has an easy way about her, even managing a smile and a laugh to break up a somber conversation. But on June 11, 1981, the day the jury came back to announce its verdict on the nineteen charges against Richard Francis Cottingham, Carol was livid. Her tone was harsh as she loudly proclaimed the eighteen-day trial of her brother a cruel farce.

Even as the trial in Judge Paul Huot's courtroom dragged on through the testimony of more than a hundred witnesses, Carol and her mother attended the court sessions with dedication and unquestioned support. With only few exceptions—such as during the lengthy testimony of Leslie Ann O'Dell—Anna took her usual seat in the front bench. It was extremely odd, therefore, that Cottingham's mother and sister could not be seen in that front row the hour the verdict was delivered.

It was 6:20 p.m. "I want to thank both of you for your cooperation," Judge Huot said to Dennis Calo, the prosecutor, and to Cottingham's lawyer, Donald Conway. "Mr. Calo," the judge continued, "the state and its citizens were well represented. Mr. Cottingham, you had a very fine defense. I want that said before the verdict comes out. I don't know what it's going to be." The twelve jurors took their seats and the court officer began the deadly serious duty of having the foreman announce decisions on each count of the indictment.

The litany began. Guilty of kidnapping Karen Schilt. Guilty of atrocious assault on Schilt. Guilty of kidnaping Susan Geiger and, likewise, of assaulting, raping, and sodomizing the nineteen-year-old. Cottingham's face was ashen, but he appeared to display little of what he was feeling. The jury foreman continued, reaching count nine, the charge of kidnapping twenty-seven-year-old Pamela Weisenfeld. "Not guilty." The words were like a trickle of water on a dying man's lips, because the next charge was for the murder of Valorie Ann Street. It was clear the jury believed Karen Schilt and Susan Geiger. They did not buy Pamela Weisenfeld's story of being kidnapped from a Manhattan bar on May 11, 1980, but much of that reasoning could have been due to Pamela's cocky attitude on the witness stand as much as the fact that her story contained too many loose ends. The devastating blow for Cottingham came with count eleven. Guilty, the jury foreman announced without hesitation. Guilty of purposely and knowingly killing a nineteen-year-old woman whom he had picked up in New York, taken to a New Jersey motel, tortured for several hours, and strangled. There was no Valorie Street to testify, but the fingerprint on the handcuffs that held the prostitute prisoner delivered the crushing blow to the Cottingham defense. On this conviction alone, he could serve twenty-five years to life in prison.

But the bad news continued, count after count. Guilty of kidnapping Leslie Ann O'Dell, of assaulting the eighteen-year-old prostitute with a knife, of brutally raping her, of sodomizing her, and of forcing the fragile young blond to perform other sexual acts. The jury had absorbed all the sordid details, measured the words and veracity of the victims and decided to believe all but one. Before he was finished, the jury foreman had told the court that he and his colleagues found Richard Cottingham guilty of fifteen of the nineteen counts in the indictment. With one count dismissed by the judge for lack of evidence and the murder charge involving

Maryann Carr severed from the rest for a separate trial, it meant the prosecutor had overwhelmingly succeeded. And if the verdicts demonstrated anything, it was the surprising fact that a group of suburban jurors would believe the stories of four women, three of them ladies of the night, over the protests of innocence of a working man and husband with three children. There was no doubt, even in the minds of the most cynical court observers, that Cottingham was guilty beyond a reasonable doubt.

Cottingham stared off into space, sitting before Judge Huot in stony silence as the weight of the verdict began to make its true burden felt. Dennis Calo, chief lawyer for the county's homicide bureau, swelled over with enthusiastic pride. The young prosecutor had not only won a major case, convincing the jury that the brutal crimes were the work of a modern-day Jack the Ripper, but he had taken on one of New Jersey's most prominent defense attorneys, an achievement that would gain him wide regard in the legal community. Surprisingly, his adversary seemed to be taking the defeat in stride. Donald R. Conway, the former president of the state Bar Association, had reached a dead end with the case. "I think the prosecutor's office worked diligently," Conway remarked in a cool but sincere concession to Calo's successful prosecution.

Judge Huot wasted little time in getting down to the next order of business. He ordered immediate revocation of Cottingham's $250,000 bail and scheduled sentencing for the fifteen convictions for September 18. Cottingham still appeared to be in a slight daze as two sheriff's officers prepared to place him in leg chains for the walk back to his jail cell. Conway was gathering his papers, catching an occasional glimpse of Calo in a warm embrace with one of his colleagues, and didn't appear to notice his client's sister and mother. Carol Jacobsen and Anna Cottingham strode up to the front row of the spectators' section, looking confused. But their perplexity very quickly turned to anger when they realized what had happened.

"I thought the family was supposed to be here," Carol declared, directing her outrage at Conway, but speaking to no one in particular. A very distressed Anna Cottingham looked as if she would faint. Her son, now shackled at his legs and hands, stoicly tried to muster a reassuring gesture to his mother, but Anna's bitterness could no longer be suppressed. "They call this a court of justice," she blurted. "I'd like to see where the justice was."

Cottingham's mother and sister learned of the jury's verdict from newsaper reporters. Mrs. Cottingham, whose first words to Donald Conway echoed the advice many troubled mothers had been given— "I heard you are the best..." —now reproached the attorney for failing to alert her that the jury had returned with its verdict. Out in the corridor, Anna's outrage continued: "Where is Conway?" she asked out loud. "He's afraid to come out. He said he's stall them [the jury], but he couldn't even do that." The grey-haired, dapperly dressed trial attorney swung open the courtroom door and started down the hallway before his exit was interrupted by Anna Cottingham. "Is that justice, that he should be standing there, alone to the world?" the defendant's mother angrily asked. Conway, well known for sardonic courtroom remarks, replied coolly: "He wasn't standing." And there ended the legal representation he'd provided Richard Cottingham. Conway, who stated just after the June 11 verdict that he would not have taken Cottingham's case if he had it to do over again, would not represent Cottingham in his pending trials. He would not even continue as legal counsel in an appeal of the Valorie Street murder verdict.

## Eleven

# The Signature Case

Not everyone who knew her considered her a sweetheart, but most would agree that Maryann Carr was a strikingly beautiful young woman with a winning smile. More beautiful than a Miss America, one close acquaintance once remarked. She was a woman whom men wanted desperately to love. And some of the men in her life wanted to be loved by her in return. There is strong reason to believe it was this second category that provided the real killer, but the state chose to prosecute Richard Cottingham.

In the twenty-six years she was alive, Maryann Carr trained and studied for a career as a radiologist, married twice, acquired a large number of friends, and decided that Bergen County, New Jersey, would be the area to settle in for life. She succeeded in her studies and worked, efficiently enough, it was said, as a medical technician for a doctor in Englewood. Maryann, a cheerleader during her four years at Tenafly High School, still had time to maintain the pace of an active circle of friends, single and married. She dated before, during, and between her two marriages. The men were always handsome-looking and eager to spend the time and money necessary to please her. Some were cops, some were doctors, and some, like Michael Carr, became involved very seriously with the stunning brunette.

Michael and Maryann had been married for little more than a year. He was a salesman on the road much of the time. The second December of their marriage saw Michael on an extended business trip to Rochester, New York. He would be gone for a more than a week and his mother, who was remarried with the name of Catherine Ferrara, promised to keep Maryann company. From the thoughts she expressed about this promise, it seemed clear that Michael's mother was doing this as much out of anxiety over Maryann's possible extramarital activities as for her son's concern over his wife's loneliness. Nevertheless, Maryann stayed one night with her mother-in-law at her home in Hackensack. That was Wednesday, December 14.

The next day, Maryann went to work at the offices of Dr. Arthur Grossman, where she and her co-worker, Dorothy Fay, put in a full schedule with the doctor's patients, a workday that ended, like most, at about seven o'clock at night. Maryann planned to return to her mother-in-law's that night about eight o'clock, but she drove her Camaro the approximate fifteen-minute ride from Dr. Grossman's through Hackensack, to her and Michael's apartment in Little Ferry. For whatever reason, the practical option of driving directly to Catherine Ferrara's was put aside, and her return home that night proved to be Maryann's last.

Ledgewood Terrace Apartments on Liberty Street in Little Ferry is a typical suburban-style, brick-faced complex of six buildings housing some seventy units with a swiming pool in the rear. Its tenants are mainly young married or single working people who share their privacy behind walls of plasterboard and wood in apartments that generally consist of one or two bedrooms, small kitchen, living room, and bath. Michael and Maryann Carr shared apartment 112 in building 462.

It was not firmly established if Maryann was with the man who resembled her husband when the two were observed next to her Camaro *before* or *after* she went inside her apartment that night. A neighbor, David Church, who lived in the same building and routinely parked his car about two spaces away from Maryann's near building 462, said he was getting into his car sometime between 7:30 and 7:40 that Thursday night. He saw Maryann standing next to her car with a man who looked like her husband Michael. It was cold and foggy, but Church felt certain that Maryann and the man he assumed to be Michael Carr were just standing there talking. Church attached no particular significance to the observation. He remembered glancing at the couple once again as he pulled his car out of the parking lot and drove off to attend his eight o'clock class at night school.

Maryann went to her apartment to shower and change out of her whites—a pair of white slacks and matching blouse—to prepare to meet her mother-in-law. On the way in, she reached down and retrieved an envelope that had been slipped under the door. It was a security check from the apartment manager. She opened it, put the check away, and left the envelope on the kitchen table. She lit a cigarette and opened the kitchen cabinet to make herself a drink. She finished neither. Nor did she ever get to change her clothes. There were no signs of a distrubance in the apartment, no indication the door had been forced open.

The only significant thing that offered any indication that something was wrong inside apartment 112 that night was brought out by a neighbor across the hallway. Jan Cousins, who lived in apartment 109, one of the four units on the second floor of the Carrs' building, said she had been lying down in her bedroom that evening. But at about 7:30, she said, she was at her front door hanging some Christmas cards. Her television was on, but the sound did not obscure the terrifying scream that came from across the hall. The neighbor was certain it came from the Carrs' apartment. Ms. Cousins had indicated some knowledge of marital problems among some of her fellow tenants. This sounded like that kind of situation, she said. She recalled only one particular scream, however, "I will . . . . I will." The words, she remembered, came from a woman, a woman she believed was Maryann Carr. Ms. Cousins recalled that she froze, nearly dumbfounded, there by her door. "I just stood at the door," she said, "not sure what to do."

When the telephone in Maryann's kitchen began ringing at about ten minutes to eight, she was either gone or unable to retrieve the phone. Catherine Ferrara, her mother-in-law, let it ring a number of times. Mrs. Ferrara said she was worried about her daughter-in-law. She had a premonition that Maryann was in trouble. Even though Maryann was not due to arrive at her Hackensack home until eight o'clock, Mrs. Ferrara said she got an urge to telephone the Little Ferry apartment. She continued dialing Maryann's number for more than three hours with the same uncomfortable result. No answer. Finally, the mother-in-law decided she'd call her nephew, Robert DeMartin, who lived in building 468 in the same apartment complex.

DeMartin, a bachelor who lived alone, calmed his aunt down and got off the telephone. Half to please her and half out of curiosity, he walked through the cold, foggy air the short distance to Maryann's building. He could see the light coming from her apartment. He pulled his building key out of his pocket, the one for building 468, and turned it in the lock on one of the four outside doors, the one closest to the Carr's apartment. He rang the doorbell, but after getting no response turned the doorknob and the door opened into a brief foyer to the living room. DeMartin noticed nothing unusual. He saw the glass, with its nearly empty contents, and a cigarette—a More brand that Maryann smoked—in an ashtray in the kitchen. Nothing seemed out of place. DeMartin said he called his aunt back and they agreed he should contact Michael Carr, who had been in Rochester since Sunday. It was after these conversations that DeMartin also called the Little Ferry police.

The Little Ferry police responded to DeMartin's call, although there was very little they could do. After all, Maryann was twenty-six years old, a married woman. Perhaps the concern over her failing to keep the appointment earlier that night with Catherine Ferrara was nothing more than the over-anxiousness of a suspicious mother-in-law. Nevertheless, Patrolman Donald Fleming went through the apartment, noticing little if anything out of the ordinary. A love seat in the living room, he noted, was moved slightly. About the only significant thing about the policeman's presence in the woman's apartment that night was a fingerprint on the glass Maryann had been drinking from. The fingerprint turned out to be Patrolman Fleming's. Fleming had picked the glass up and handled it enough to smudge other prints and leave his own.

The Little Ferry police did make an important observation the night Maryann Carr was reported missing, however. At some point of the early morning hours of December 16, a police patrol noticed a reddish-orange Camaro parked in the area of building 470 at the Ledgewood Terrace Apartments. Patrolman Von Rudenborg hadn't the slightest idea of the importance of that observation. He couldn't have known that the Camaro, which was Maryann's, would subsequently be cited in a broad range of circumstantial findings. Certainly the police did not know, and at the time probably wouldn't have paid any attention to the fact, that Richard Cottingham had once lived in building 470.

More than four years had elapsed since those events of December 15 and December 16, 1977, but some law enforcement officials continued to wonder exactly where Maryann Carr went that night, or, more accurately, where she was taken. That's why, on the morning of February 22, 1981, in a secret session with Superior Court Judge James F. Madden, Dennis Calo, still exuberant over his success in prosecuting Cottingham in the Valorie Street murder, wanted desperately to hear a step-by-step account of the strangled nurse's last hours. What Calo proposed to Cottingham and his new defense attorney, Frank Wagner, wasn't actually a plea bargain in the usual sense of the concept, although the press, because of a slip made by Judge Madden later that morning in open court, interpreted it that way. It was more of an appeal agreement.

The state was proceeding with a prosecution of Cottingham, using a wide array of circumstantial evidence that it claimed would put Cottingham's signature on the murder of Maryann Carr. But Calo knew that Wagner would appeal a conviction based on that kind of evidence, and he needed a guarantee that the New Jersey Supreme Court would not be asked to review the conviction if he won it. So the prosecutor said he was authorized to pledge that the Bergen County Prosecutor would not press an appeal in the case if the state lost with an acquital of the homicide charge against Cottingham. He would make this pledge in return for Cottingham's promise to do likewise: no apeal to the Supreme Court if a jury or a judge finds Cottingham guilty of murdering the twenty-six-year-old nurse. But Calo wanted something else. He needed more, much more. Because the state, with all the witnesses (at least fifty-seven would be called for the Carr case) and the wealth of evidence (more than 185 items would be marked into evidence) that would be presented to support its "signature" theory, did not know for certain where the murder happened, when it happened, or why it happened. And these crucial factors remained a real mystery, not only to the prosecutor, whose theory it was that Cottingham was responsible for the Carr murder, but to some court observers who wondered about the motivations of the prosecutors.

What Calo wanted was a statement from Cottingham that would essentially plug the gaps in the prosecutor's case. Cottingham was to detail how, why, when, and where he slipped a thin ligature around Maryann's slender neck and pulled it ever so tightly, causing her lungs to collapse. The autopsy, performed by Dr. John Aprovian, the assistant Bergen County medical examiner, placed the approximate time of death at about three hours before her body was discovered by a patron outside the Quality Inn Motel in Hasbrouck Heights. Even Dr. Aprovian, who ultimately returned with a far different approach to his theory of method, was a little off in some of his calculations, however. His placing of the time of death at about 4:15 a.m. on Friday, December 16, was open to debate.

Aprovian initially reported that Maryann was strangled with her necklace before her body was dumped in some shrubbery near a chain-link fence behind the motel. The following day, which was Saturday, County Prosecutor Roger W. Breslin, Jr., held a news conference to announce, among other things, that Mrs. Carr had been smothered. Dr. Aprovian, Breslin explained, had changed his opinion on the cause of death to suffocation, a conclusion apparently based on the fact that the autopsy showed that her lungs had collapsed. However, in his final analysis. Dr. Aprovian not only changed his theory back to strangulation, but he opined that whatever instrument was used—a strap, rope, wire, or even a necklace—the ligature was pulled from the left side.

Cottingham's statement would, of course, answer a lot of other questions. David Church, the young man who lived in Maryann's building, thought he saw her with her husband, Michael, the night before her body was found. After learning that Michael Carr was a good five-and-a-half-hour car trip away that night in Rochester, New York, Church must have wondered who he had observed standing and talking to Mrs. Carr in the apartment building parking lot. And Jan Cousins, who thought she heard a heated marital exchange of unintelligible words in apartment 112 across the hallway where the Carrs had lived for more than fifteen months, certainly would be curious enough to want to know what Maryann was indicating she would do when she screamed, "I will. . . I will." The statement might also tell Little Ferry Patrolman Donald Fleming whether anyone else was inside Maryann's apartment that night, the night his investigation of her whereabouts was so routinely conducted that he left his fingerprints on a glass and God only knows what else.

What Calo intended to do with Cottingham's statement of his activities during the time frame of Maryann's last sighting by David Church and when she ended up lying face down in a clump of shrubbery outside a motel is subject to speculation. The private session with Cottingham, before Judge Madden, lasted about two hours, but Calo did not indicate that he would use the statement against the defendant. In fact, the agreement was to contain the important clause that Cottingham's statement would not be presented in court. Hypothetically, if Cottingham did make the statement and agreed to put it in the form of a sworn affidavit, there is one way the prosecutor might get it into the record of a trial. Cottingham had taken the witness stand in his own defense in the previous trial, even in the face of such overwhelming evidence as his being caught in the same motel where he had (allegedly until he was proven guilty) just beaten and sexually tortured Leslie Ann O'Dell. He might also testify in the pending trial. If he did testify and Calo saw just a slight discrepancy from the sworn statement, the prosecutor might raise a perjury charge and use it as an additional wedge to convict Cottingham for the Carr murder. Again, this is only speculation, but one could seriously question just for what purpose the prosecutor wanted that statement. Any speculation is academic, however. Cottingham refused to make such a statement, even in the face of the prosecution's pledge not to pursue the charge if its case was dismissed.

Calo's intriguing appeal arrangement offer was not the first agreement the government sought with Richard Cottingham, and it was certainly not to be the last, as this convicted murderer looked ahead to more trials in New York. Sentenced to between 173 to 197 years for one murder, three kidnappings, and various sexual assault and drug-related convictions, Cottingham was sent to Trenton Prison, New Jersey's largest and most secure penitentiary. On those terms alone, he would stay inside for at least forty years before he was eligible for parole. About a month after Judge Paul Huot announced the nearly 200-year sentence on July 26, 1981, Frank Wagner, the county public defender who took over Cottingham's defense after Donald Conway refused to continue the legal relationship, received a plea bargain offer. It was a joint arrangement between Bergen County and the office of Manhattan

District Attorney Robert Morgenthau, under which Cottingham would admit to the murder of Maryann Carr and two of the three New York murders. Cottingham was charged with the two mutilation murders that occurred in New York in December, 1979; one of the victims was Deedah Goodarzi, while the other has never been identified. He had also been indicted for the May 15, 1980, strangulation murder of Mary Ann "Jean" Reyner. Morgenthau's office did not specify which of the three murders would be dismissed, but it was assumed it was the murder of Goodarzi's fellow victim, identified only as Case Number 79-8105. The offer came at a meeting August 17, between Wagner, Calo, and Nancy E. Ryan, an assistant to District Attorney Morgenthau.

But a good month before the plea bargain meeting, Nancy Ryan wrote a lengthy letter to one of Cottingham's former defense counselors, the junior partner of Donald Conway, Peter E. Doyne. The information contained in Ryan's letter—from a dubious source, it turned out—could have served a crushing blow to the New York indictment.

The dubious source was James Nicholas Jellicks, a former police informant and undercover operative, who had made a career of getting out of tight spots with the law by selling street information, mostly about drug buys. Jellicks, described variously as a forger and a break and entry expert, was working as an undercover operative for the New Jersey State Police in 1977, the year Maryann Carr was murdered, in the state's investigation of drugging and race fixing at Freehold Raceway. Along the way he broke into a stable at the Colts Neck horse farm owned by Carmine Abbatiello. Unfortunately for Jellicks, he was caught red-handed. The incident mushroomed into a full-blown investigation of state police hiring and use of such informants, and Jellicks was put out in the cold when he told investigators from the New Jersey State Commission of Investigation that he was put up to the Abbatiello break-in by his employer, Colonel Clinton Pagano, the state police superintendant. Jellicks, once used as an informant and witness in government prosecutions, was characterized as a "pathological liar" by Colonel Pagano, who pressed the burglary charge and had Jellicks put away for six months for the offense.

In 1980, Jellicks, a slight, wiry figure of a man who was born and raised in the rough-and-tumble neighborhoods of Jersey City, was in Staten Island, in the middle of an armed robbery at a supermarket, when events brought him to the Queens County House of Detention. There he got to know a fellow Jersey City native being held for trial in the brutal murder of a nineteen-year-old Jackson Heights, Queens, woman. Jellicks told Queens authorities that this friend, a forty-one-year-old cab driver, had confided in him about mutilating two prostitutes at the Travel Inn on Times Square. The cab driver, Jellicks told authorities, "expressed relief over the fact that Cottingham had been arrested for the killings because otherwise the police might have gotten him." Cottingham was charged with the two Travel Inn murders in an indictment disclosed on August 4, 1980. In her letter of July 16, 1981, Ryan said Jellicks offered further information for New York investigators, still perplexed over the whereabouts of the heads and hands of the two Times Square victims. Jellicks, according to Ryan's letter, said the cab driver "told him he had disposed of the heads in Jersey City by Route 440." That section of Jersey City, near the Pulaski Skyway, is also where federal agents searched the rubble of garbage in Phil "Brother" Moscato's dump for the remains of Jimmy Hoffa, the Teamsters union leader whose disappearance in 1975 remains unsolved. Ms. Ryan also said that Jellicks' story furnished other information about the two murders.

Wagner, the head of Bergen County's ten-lawyer public defender's office, met twice with Cottingham in the month before he was sentenced for the Street murder conviction on July 26. The discussions mainly centered on Cottingham's response to a plea bargain on the Carr homicide and the pending New York charges. Miss Ryan's July 16 letter was sent to Peter Doyne as part of the requirements of discovery, when the prosecutor must provide the defense lawyers with information that is exculpatory, or may help the accused prove his or her innocence. Doyne indicated he had forwarded Ms. Ryan's July 16 letter to Cottingham at Trenton State Prison.

However, Wagner later related that neither he nor his client had knowledge of the Jellicks story when the two met in July to consider pleading guilty to the murders that some forty-one-year-old Jersey City taxi driver had purportedly confessed to committing. Doyne claims to have fulfilled his responsibilities: "My obligation is to Mr. Cottingham, not to Mr. Wagner." After the Jellicks information became public, Doyne said he would pass the Ryan letter on to Cottingham's new lawyer. The Manhattan District Attorney's office, especially Ms. Ryan, insisted they had no legal obligation to forward discovery material to Wagner; the New York cases were not before a trial judge. But keeping in mind that they were communicating and meeting with Frank Wagner to arrange a plea from Cottingham on two of the Manhattan murders, one could surely surmise that a prisoner's purported confession to two of the murders would and should have become part of the discussion. Ms. Ryan simply contended that the Jellicks episode had no relevance because the former police informant's story had been investigated, the cab driver's confession had been dismissed as untrue, and New York had no plans to drop the three homicide counts against Cottingham.

Wagner, however, advised his client to reject the joint plea bargain offer. While Ryan's office may have been willing, apparently with no little influence from the fact that Jellicks had a psychiatric history and an extensive criminal background, to forget that someone else may have committed the mutilation slayings, Wagner indicated there was more to the purported confession that his office would have to pursue. And, finally, Dennis Calo, who was prepared to prosecute the Maryann Carr case, claimed to know nothing about the reported confession to the Times Square murders. Nor did the assistant county prosecutor express the least astonishment at the attitude of his colleagues in Manhattan: "I suppose New York never gave it credence. I don't give it credence, either."

But if Dennis Calo was certain New York authorities had ample evidence to convict Richard Cottingham for the mutilation murders of Deedah Goodarzi and Ms. X and the stabbing and burning of Jean Reyner, the assistant prosecutor was not as confident that the evidence he had directly connecting Cottingham to the murder of Maryann Carr was enough to convince a jury, or a judge, to close the 1977 murder case with a guilty verdict. Reminded constantly of the state's awesome burden to prove a defendant's guilt, Calo would have to gather together all the devastating circumstantial evidence he had from Cottingham's criminal history. If he couldn't put the murder squarely on the then thirty-five-year-old defendant's shoulders, the prosecutor would have to use other tactics and means to prove his theory. He wouldn't be able to place Cottingham at Maryann's side, there where her body was found in a deserted parking area of the Quality Inn Motel. Such direct evidence, a fingerprint or two, just was not available. But the prosecutor could heap a truckload of other testimony before the jury, evidence that Cottingham was a viciously perverted man who conducted a one-man war to seek out and punish women, especially promiscuous women.

In New Jersey, there is a perfectly legal, if sometimes unfair and judiciously questionable, means to accomplish the prosecutor's goal. It is incorporated in the state's criminal code and court law as Rule 55, found under the section on the rules of evidence. Simply stated, Rule 55 permits the presentation of testimony or evidence pertaining to the defendant's prior criminal history. The circumstances or facts raised in the Rule 55 testimony must be relevant to at least one of several critical issues: the motive, plan, or identity presented as the defendant's from the previous crimes must have definite correlative value to proving that the individual who committed the prior criminal acts is the same person charged in the present matter on trial.

For example, let's say that Joe Dokes, a thirty-year-old carpenter convicted previously for raping Linda Doe, is indicted for murdering twenty-two-year-old Mary Smith. Her body, found in a shallow grave in a desolate area of rural New York State, was so decomposed and gutted by wild animals that medical authorities could not determine if Ms. Smith was sexually assaulted. But the body did reveal evidence that the victim was strangled by powerfully strong hands and in such a way that a medical expert could actually determine that one hand was placed at the back of the woman's neck, while a ligature, probably her pantyhose, was pulled against her Adam's apple. The technique was not odd, but uncommon.

It so happened that before Joe Dokes raped Linda Doe, the twenty-eight-year-old sexual assault victim whose identification of Dokes was crucial in convicting him in a previous trial, he grabbed the victim around the neck, placing one hand at the back of her neck. On the request of the prosecutor, the trial judge in the Smith murder case holds a hearing out of the presence of the jury, and then decides to allow the state to call Ms. Doe as a witness in the murder trial. Ms. Doe, obviously still scarred by the brutal experience of being raped just a few years prior by Dokes, relates her story in graphic language and with great emotion, at the end pointing to the murder defendant, Mr. Dokes, as her rapist.

Now, there is just one last, but nevertheless highly important technical point with regard to the jury's review of Ms. Doe's testimony. The jurors are instructed to listen to her describe how the hands were placed around her neck, keeping in mind to note what similarities are critical to the murder of Ms. Smith. And, of course, they are to consider that the witness is able to identify Dokes as her attacker. But the jury is supposed to be instructed not to infer from Ms. Doe's testimony that, merely because Dokes was her rapist, the defendant is automatically guilty of murder. The jurors are to weigh the importance of the similarities between the method used to hold Ms. Doe around the neck and the way Ms. Smith was strangled. If it was the same, or so nearly the same, method, the signature of the deadly handiwork may be that of Joe Dokes and it can add substantially to the weight of other evidence.

It can be a very difficult mental exercise for jurors, but with proper instruction from the judge, the testimony on motive, plan, and/or identify is supposed to assist the jury in deciding if the defendant is the type of person capable of planning and executing such a crime. Critics, and there are many, might say the exercise is not unlike a judge's admonishing a jury to disregard a remark from a witness that is clearly prejudicial. It is difficult to imagine how anyone could actually erase such remarks from his memory. It is equally difficult to believe that a juror, after listening to Ms. Doe's tearful recollections of being sexually attacked, will not be prone to prejudge Mr. Dokes before all the evidence is considered.

If the prosecution team encountered any major roadblock in their journey to put Richard Cottingham before a jury for Maryann Carr's murder, it didn't happen during the investigation. Nor did it occur because of the preeminent reputation of Donald R. Conway or anyone connected with his defense team. The baton had been handed to the tax-supported county public defender's office and to Frank Wagner, an able lawyer and a thorn in the side of the Bergen County prosecutor's office. Because of Wagner's persistence, the prosecutor had never succeeded in convicting Robert Ronald Reldan, whose double-murder indictment and the trial, based heavily on the so-called Rule 55 evidence procedure, would return —on appeal—to haunt the prosecutor. But still it wasn't Wagner's same stubborn insistence on providing good counsel to even the likes of a rapist-murderer like Richard Cottingham that proved to be the most difficult challenge to Dennis Calo and his associates. The major trouble came from Paul Robert Huot.

Superior Court Judge Paul Huot had been on the bench fifteen years when he got the Cottingham cases in 1981. And although he'd been in the judicial circles all that time, he never joined the club or subscribed to its cronyism. Quiet, reserved, even to a fault of being aloof, Huot, nevertheless, won the higher marks of an excellent jurist the hard way. "Some judges are so afraid they're going to be appealed that they bend over backwards," one prominent attorney told a profile writer for *The New York Times*, "but Judge Huot is independent. He runs a tight courtroom." So high was the regard for his fairness and strict regard for proper rules of procedure and evidence that Judge Huot was selected to preside over one of New Jersey's most controversial and politically volatile trials.

When Kenneth A. Gibson, mayor of Newark, the state's largest city, and one of a handful of black politicians in the nation to hold such a post, came to trial for permitting a no-show employee to remain on the city's payroll, Judge Huot was selected to preside. He had certainly learned a few lessons from having handled Cottingham's cases. One of the remarks that was most telling of his attitude toward attorneys for the state came at a point in the Gibson trial when John A Matthews 3rd, the prosecutor, tried to discredit one of his own witnesses after the man had testified that Mayor Gibson could not have known the no-show employee lived in Florida. Judge Huot beckoned the prosecutor to the bench and, with the jury out of the courtroom, started in on what he, the judge, felt was wrong with Matthews' performance. "It sounds to me like what I have heard so far in this case is that you have started with a preconceived judgment and you are trying to weave everything into this. I'm looking for some direct evidence." It was not surprising that the jury voted to acquit Mayor Gibson.

About two months after Judge Huot sentenced Cottingham for the murder of Valorie Ann Street and the kidnapping convictions, the prosecution made known its intentions to put Cottingham's "signature" on the 1977 strangulation of Maryann Carr. Assistant Prosecutor Calo would try to obtain a conviction by pointing out the similarities between the 1980 strangulation of Valorie Street and that of Mrs. Carr, a married nurse. The Street-Carr theory, Calo would argue, was based on three significant parallels: the use of adhesive tape, handcuffs, and the strangulation. In order to present such a comparison, Calo had to persuade Huot to permit not only the evidence presented in the 1981 trial pertaining to the strangled nineteen-year-old prostitute, but also the testimony of the three women who identified Cottingham as their abductor and much of the mountain of evidence used to win the June 11, 1981, convictions for those crimes. Judge Huot agreed to hold a so-called

Rule 8 hearing, which brings out the testimony and evidence the prosecutor wants included in the Rule 55 exception so the defense can make its opposition known and the court can rule on its admissibility or reject the prosecutor's request.

On the morning of October 19, Judge Huot scheduled a session with Assistant Prosecutor Calo and Public Defender Wagner before him to announce the court's decision on the Rule 55 request. It was obvious from the start that Judge Huot was not in one of his better moods. After all, he had been reviewing a voluminous trial transcript and about 165 pieces of evidence presented in the Street murder case. "Good morning, gentlemen," the judge greeted Calo and Wagner from the bench. "I spent the weekend reading, comparing, reviewing, thinking, and writing. I hope you enjoyed your weekend." The judge briefly reviewed the prosecutor's Rule 55 application to present evidence from Cottingham's trial involving the murdered prostitute and the other women, Karen Schilt, Susan Geiger, and Leslie Ann O'Dell. Adopted by the state Supreme Court in 1967 and included in the criminal code's provisions for trial evidence, the provision permits a narrow field of evidence from other criminal convictions "to prove some other fact in issue including motive, intent, plan, knowledge, identity, or absence of mistake or accident." Judge Huot noted that Calo's request was based on the state's contention that the Street evidence was necessary to prove Cottingham's identity with a specific modus operandi. As Calo's boss, Prosecutor Roger W. Breslin, Jr., put it, "without the Rule 55 evidence, the state will have a very difficult time proving its case."

Briefly, here is what Calo set forth in his argument to admit evidence from the other convictions: "There is only one real issue in the Maryann Carr case: Who abducted and killed the young woman. Simply stated, the state considers Richard Cottingham's modus operandi as so unique, novel, and dissimilar as to be strictly personal to himself." But the young assistant prosecutor plunged into the mound of evidence, coming up with supposed similarities by the shovelful. Judging from Huot's response, Calo would have been better off using a teaspoon.

Calo listed nine items of similarity between Karen Schilt, the twenty-two-year-old housewife Cottingham abducted in 1978, and Maryann Carr, including their physical description. For instance, Calo contended both women had artificially treated blond hair, but Huot said his examination of samples showed Mrs. Carr's hair to be much darker. Another obvious similarity in the crimes was the fact that Karen Schilt was found in the parking lot of Ledgewood Terrace apartments in Little Ferry, where it was believed Maryann was abducted. Judge Huot did not like the idea the prosecutor was trying to plant with the jury. "We do not know, we may only infer that Maryann Carr was taken from that lot," Huot stated. "But, even if she was so taken, Ledgewood Terrace does not constitute a signature. It is an apartment complex with six buildings of seventy-two apartments; many people live and have lived there; inferentially, many people visit there and many more would pass it on the public street that abuts the apartment." In another point, Calo tried to claim that both women received a "beating" at the hand of their abductor. However, Judge Huot responded that the medical reports showed one minor bruise on one of Maryann's breasts and discoloration on the upper part of her forehead that the medical examiner determined was caused by trauma. Calo also tried to say that both Karen Schilt and Maryann Carr were robbed. "Carr's ring and chain, valuable possessions, remained on her body," Judge Huot noted, "and there is no evidence to indicate that she had a handbag with her that particular evening."

Assistant Prosecutor Calo's ninth and last item of "similarity" between Karen and Maryann was that Cottingham punished them because they were promiscuous. Promiscuity was argued as a similarity in each of the cases, including the three prostitutes, who, because of their profession, made the state's theory more plausible. But Judge Huot took a dim view of comparing Schilt's and the others' virtues to those of Maryann Carr. "The argument is the defendant's perception of victims as promiscuous whom he must punish, and I find that here the state is really straining," the judge stated. Huot was thoroughly familiar with Cottingham's history, including some of its most seamy aspects. For the sake of argument, the judge said Cottingham might consider nurses to be promiscuous, certainly there was a strong indication that he considered them an easy mark. But, Huot continued, "there is nothing to indicate the state's conclusion that he [Cottingham] wanted to punish them, even accepting the state's hypothesis that defendant wanted to punish prostitutes, it does not follow as to nurses."

Judge Huot also noted that Cottingham dated Barbara Lucas and that there was no indication from her testimony that Cottingham ever punished her. In fact, Cottingham's extramarital relations included two nurses: Barbara, who was a registered nurse at Bellevue Hospital, and Jean Connelly, who worked at Monte Fiore Hospital, both in New York. Jean started seeing Cottingham in early 1980 until just before his arrest in May. Barbara dated him from 1977 to the time he went to jail in 1980. Neither of the two nurses complained of being beaten or punished, although Barbara Lucas didn't particularly appreciate the books Cottingham would recommend. About the only complaint Barbara registered was that their sexual relations became habitual and with few surprises, although she did say they were satisfying.

Calo made the point again about promiscuity in comparing Susan Geiger's kidnapping and attack, and again Judge Huot dismissed the proposition. "Now, this may be true," he said, "with respect to Geiger as a prostitute, it may be true with respect to Schilt in being perceived as a loose woman because she was in a bar on Third Avenue in New York late at night by herself. That does not apply to Maryann Carr."

"After picking these women up," Judge Huot continued, "he would travel to New Jersey. Geiger, Street and O'Dell were taken to motels where they were sexually assaulted and savagely treated. Schilt was not taken to a motel, but she was sexually and savagely assaulted. Schilt and Geiger were left for dead, Street was in fact left dead, and O'Dell was lucky she screamed. But with Maryann Carr the pattern does not fit .... no evidence to indicate that she was promiscuous. The state's argument that [the] defendant perceived her a nurse and that all nurses were promiscuous and therefore sought to harm her is speculative imagination."

Judge Huot rejected all seven items of similarity argued by Calo in Susan Geiger's case, but the judge did accept three points of similarity in Valorie Street's murder and two points made to compare the abduction and beating of Leslie Ann O'Dell with issues in the Carr murder. Both prostitutes were handcuffed and both had their mouths sealed shut with adhesive tape. Both Street and Carr, according to medical records, had been strangled. On the point of strangulation, Judge Huot still maintained his skepticism, however:

"The tenth item in the state's brief is that both [Street and Carr] were strangled, and that part is true. However, it is also to be noted as I evaluate that strangulation that Dr. [Louis V.] Napolitano opined that the strap, rope, or wire was tightened from the right side, that appears in [medical examiner's report and testimony] of the Street murder, while Dr. [John] Aprovian opined as to Carr that it was pulled from the left side. While both were strangled, there is that difference that appears on the record, and that I will have to consider."

But Judge Huot accepted three "significant similarities" between the Valorie Street and Maryann Carr cases: the use of tape to bind the victims' mouths; the use of handcuffs on their hands and feet; and the strangulation. However, Huot, adhering to his code of fairness and with a healthy sense of skepticism about the similarities asserted by the prosecutor, went on to list four major dissimilarities found in the Street-Carr murders:

- Valorie Ann Street was a prostitute working the streets of New York. Maryann Carr was a medical technician, married, and living with her husband in a suburban apartment complex. "Someone came to her door or accosted her in the parking lot;

whichever it was, however, it is different from picking up a prostitute in New York."

- Valorie Street was the victim of savagery. She had a large bruise on the right side of her head, bruises on her right shoulder, right arm, and left armpit, and her breasts were lacerated by a sharp instrument and the nipples were severely bitten. She had three cuts to the sternum, one cut to the abdomen, and, finally, she had a blood-alcohol reading of .216 percent. "The injury to Carr was in no way comparable. Of particular importance is that there were no bite marks or other signs of savagery to the breasts and there was no blood-alcohol content."
- Both Valorie Street and Leslie O'Dell were sexually assaulted. Leslie testified to intercourse, sodomy, and fellatio; vaginal, anal, and oral swabs from Valorie Street disclosed seminal material. "There was apparently no sexual activity with Carr."
- The judge noted that Cottingham never abducted a female whom he did not ply with alcohol and drugs. Valorie Street's blood samples showed strong traces of alcohol and two powerful tranquilizers, Amobarbital and Secobarbital. Leslie Ann O'Dell did not have much alcohol in her blood, but she was "sweet-talked" with promises of help and money to return her to her parents' home in Washington. "Carr had no alcohol or drugs in her system, as I say, [and] there's no evidence of any association prior to or on that night [she was abducted]."

In conclusion, Judge Huot, who had presided over the eighteen-day trial and had listened to all the testimony and studied each piece of evidence presented before Cottingham was convicted of strangling Valorie Street and abducting the other three, ruled that nothing from the crimes involving the four women could be admitted in the state's direct case against Cottingham. The similarities, when weighed against the "very substantial dissimilarities cannot be held to be so nearly identical in method as to earmark the crime against Carr as defendant's handiwork. The court cannot find the modus operandi so unusual and distinctive that it constitutes a signature."

The ruling was a stunning, if only temporary, setback to Assistant Prosecutor Dennis Calo and his office. Calo's written argument, submitted to Huot in a thick brief, concluded that if his case was denied the testimony and evidence from the Street case, it would be impossible to proceed with Cottingham's trial for Maryann Carr's murder. But Calo was determined to proceed. The next set of events demonstrated that determination; and the juggling of motions and the planning and tactical maneuvers also demonstrated why the public is skeptical—and sometimes justifiably so—that court justice is always fair.

The prosecutor took Judge Huot's decision to a New Jersey appeals court; specifically, to the three-judge panel that sits in Hackensack and which included Judge Theodore W. Trautwein, the former Bergen County Assignment Judge. The two other judges were John W. Fritz and John L. Ard. In its decision, released ten days after Judge Huot's ruling, the appeals court panel reversed Huot, saying the evidence used to convict Cottingham before could be admitted again. It was a surprising and curious ruling both because of the speed with which it was readied and delivered and, most important, because it was an odd result to see that three judges made such a crucial decision without backing it up with a full written opinion, detailing their reasons for reversing Judge Huot, who himself called the ruling surprising. "This kind of decision is surprising to anyone when they [the appeals court] reverse a court's opinion on the merits," an angry Frank Wagner declared, noting the lack of reasons for the reversal. The ball was back in Wagner's court. The public defender filed notice with the New Jersey Supreme Court, asking the state's highest court to intervene. But on November 12, 1981, in a unanimous decision, the Supreme Court refused to hear Cottingham's appeal. The state's highest tribunal gave no reasons for its decision, but ordered Bergen County to move ahead with its trial.

Assistant Prosecutor Calo's next move was bold, but predictable. With a major victory in hand, the prosecutor went back before Judge Huot and asked the balding, fifty-four-year-old jurist to step down from the Cottingham case. Calo argued that since a higher court had overruled him on the crucial question of certain evidence and because Judge Huot would now be permitting the admission of evidence contrary to his own opinion, Huot should disqualify himself. Huot reminded the young prosecutor that the jury, not the trial judge, weighs the evidence. Nevertheless, Judge Huot, who had already been requested by the defense to step down, did accede to the prosecutor's motion and agreed to disqualify himself to leave no question of the possibility of an appeal because of his strong objection to allowing a jury to hear the circumstantial evidence. But he didn't leave the case without some final remarks. "If this matter were not so serious it would be amusing," Huot said, noting that the public defender was not asking him to stay, but was at the same time objecting to Calo's plea as an effort to go "judge shopping." "I must be doing something right," Huot continued, "since both of you want me out. What members of the bar—defense and prosecution—are showing to the public is not a concern for impartial judgment, but [that] lawsuits have become contests for gladiators."

Frank Wagner wanted Judge Huot "out," as the judge put it, not because of the judge's opinions or abilities; the defense wanted the Maryann Carr murder case out of Bergen County. Cottingham's jailing, the investigation, the indictment, the lengthy Street trial testimony, and all the maneuvering with appeals had kept the former Lodi resident, the father of three young children, on the minds of the county's citizens, who were bombarded with coverage from New Jersey and New York newspapers and television. Wagner, fearful of pretrial publicity influencing a jury, particularly one selected from among Bergen County residents, wanted the trial moved to another county; if that was refused, the public defender would ask that a foreign jury, one made up of residents from another county, be empanelled in Hackensack for the second trial. As it turned out, the defense was doubly rebuffed. The assignment judge, Judge Arthur Simpson, one week after Judge Huot's self-disqualification, selected a new judge to sit in Hackensack and begin the trial January 25, 1982. The new judge was James F. Madden, who would begin the trial in February only to have it end in a mistrial because of Cottingham's collapse from a bleeding ulcer.

In the short period—all of three days—that Richard Cottingham was before Judge James F. Madden for the 1977 murder, two significant things occurred. One would not unfold for several months, but the first indicated how Bergen County would proceed with this five-year-old murder case.

Several hours elapsed after the designated 10 a.m. hearing on February 22 was to begin. Members of the press waited in the hallway outside Judge Madden's courtroom. A sheriff's deputy mentioned something about the defendant needing a pair of shoes before he could appear in court. But as the morning began to close in on noon-hour, it was clear that something more significant than the defendant's proper attire was brewing. Just after the lunch recess, Judge Madden appeared in court and the attorneys seated themselves as the deputies escorted Cottingham into the courtroom.

Madden called the pretrial session to order and Frank Wagner rose to make two requests. First, he said, Cottingham wants a nonjury trial, because of the "great potential of prejudice" if a jury is selected in Bergen County. In a nonjury trial, the judge not only presides over what is admitted into evidence, but also reviews the testimony and evidence, weighs it and makes a conclusion on guilt or innocence. Such procedure is not unusual for highly technical federal criminal cases, and, occasionally, state court cases are heard by a judge. But it is a very uncommon occurrence in murder cases. Knowledgeable court observors say such a trial proceeding has never happened in a homicide case in Bergen County.

But Judge Madden, suggesting greater faith in the jury selection process than did defense attorney Wagner, rejected the nonjury trial request. Among other things, Madden acknowledged that just that morning he became aware of a plea bargain offer made by Assistant Prosecutor Calo. Actually, while the judge was exercising extreme caution for the sake of appearances, there was nothing prejudicial about the plea bargain negotiations that occurred that morning between Calo and Wagner, with Cottingham present. Calo wanted Cottingham to sign a statement—a confession, in reality—detailing how he killed Maryann Carr. Since Cottingham refused, certainly there was nothing the judge could have heard or seen that would influence an opinion about Cottingham's guilt, at least not from the plea bargain talks. Wagner's second request, made in expectation of the judge's decision not to hear the case nonjury, was to have the jury sequestered during the trial. This too was denied, and Madden directed that the first pool of potential jurors be brought into courtroom to begin the tedious selection process.

The defense and prosecution lawyers were into their third day of interviewing potential jurors, with just twelve persons held aside for further challenges, when the shocking news spread through the courthouse. Richard Cottingham, who had appeared stout, if just slightly pale, from his incarceration, had collapsed while being escorted to his jailcell. The defendant was taken to the county hospital where a physician diagnosed his gastric disorder as a duodenal ulcer. Part of his small intestine was inflamed and bleeding. The prognosis was uncertain, but Judge Madden was advised that the defendant would need bed rest and medication. He would not be able to stand trial for at least two weeks and possibly a month might be lost. Judge Madden called the attorneys to his courtroom on February 25 and called a mistrial.

# Twelve

# Finding a New Judge

In December of 1977, Richard Cottingham was living with his wife, Janet, and their three young children, in a rented Cape Cod home at 29 Vreeland Street in Lodi, New Jersey, about a thirty-minute drive from New York City. At the same time, Cottingham was seeing at least one other woman on a regular basis. She was Barbara Lucas, a nurse who lived in Manhattan. Among the things they did together included a few visits to a nearby motel, the Quality Inn in Hasbrouck Heights, the next town over from Lodi. The first of their overnight visits to the motel came in the summer of 1977, when, as Barbara put it, the couple was planning a trip to Pennsylvania, but it got late and "we decided to get a room for the night."

Also in 1977, Cottingham had a friend and co-worker by the name of John Van Soest. Van Soest lived in New York and was anxious to move to the suburbs. Cottingham, who had known Van Soest for several years while the two men worked together in the computer department at Blue Cross and Blue Shield of Greater

New York, recommended a place where he and his wife once lived, an apartment complex in Little Ferry, a short bus or car commute to downtwon Manhattan. The Cottinghams lived at the apartments, called Ledgewood Terrace, on Liberty Street in Little Ferry, just off Route 46, in the early 1970's until about the middle of 1974, when they moved into the house in Lodi. Van Soest liked the idea very much. He had a lot of expensive recording equipment—a hobby of his was sound recording—and he didn't like the poor security of his New York apartment. Ledgewood Terrace sounded a whole lot nicer and safer. Ironically, not long after his move, Van Soest's apartment in Building 462 of the complex was broken into and robbed. The thief or thieves left the place in a mess, with furniture slashed and shelves and cabinets ransacked. It wasn't an ordinary break and entry; certainly not the clean, quiet work of an expert.

Barbara Lucas may have felt it strange the way Richard insisted they enter the Hasbrouck Heights motel from the rear door. . . .

John Van Soest probably wondered why anyone would bother stealing a set of keys that included one key that opened the outside door to his apartment building in the Ledgewood Terrace complex. . . .

Janet Cottingham, the loving faithful wife, of course, knew nothing of the love affair her husband was having with Barbara Lucas. She also knew very little or nothing of her husband's gambling trips to Atlantic City or his loansharking activities. And Janet had no idea in 1977 that some of the money her husband was withholding from her and their children was being paid to hookers for his aberrent sexual pleasures.

As for Richard, who in 1977 was feeling a new sense of freedom to experiment in his life-long sexual fantasies, never in his wildest imaginings would he have thought that those visits to the Quality Inn with Barbara and that the key stolen from John Van Soest would some day become the center of a web of circumstances that would convict him for the murder of Maryann Carr.

In the more than two years he had been in prison or jail since his arrest in May of 1980, Richard Cottingham had tried twice to take his own life; conspired with other inmates in an ill-fated plan to break out of the Bergen County Jail; and had collapsed in pain from a bleeding ulcer that put him in a hospital bed for several weeks and caused yet another long delay to his on-going court appearances. He had also twice refused to admit to any of the murders. He was particularly adamant in his rejection of the special plea offer made by Assistant Prosecutor Calo. Weaker physically—his hulking 187 pounds had shrunk to about 170 after prison medical authorities put him on a special diet to control the growth of his ulcer—Cottingham seemed as stoic as ever. He was no longer meekly willing to let his attorney do all his talking, although he consistently refused to do any talking outside the courtoom. Even in the courtroom appearances since his June 11, 1981, multiple convictions, he stood his ground, still denying all charges, except those related to the eighteen-year-old prostitute Leslie Ann O'Dell.

"The first time I did get convicted on being a bad guy rather than the facts of the case." Cottingham, again before a judge in October 1982, still insisted that it was the events of May 22, 1980, that caused the jury in his 1981 trial to convict him for strangling Valorie Ann Street. Now the defendant was before a new judge for his second trial and he was pleading to have the evidence heard by the judge, not a jury. Judge James F. Madden, who denied the nonjury trial request back in February, had been relieved of the murder trial because of his conflicting court schedule. Summer, with its long court recess for vacations, had passed and Cottingham was now before Judge Fred C. Galda in Hackensack.

Galda, the criminal assignment court judge, had agreed to hear the case himself. He became the third trial court judge to have Cottingham before him. Galda, affable and outgoing when he was off the bench talking to lawyers or courthouse visitors, was intent and serious as he listened to Cottingham and his attorney, Frank Wagner, argue the negative effects of empanelling a jury for the Maryann Carr case.

Having failed in the effort to move the trial outside the county, Wagner's strategy was to by-pass the jury process. He pointed out that when the matter was before Judge Madden, eighty-three of the persons in the ninety-five-member pool of potential jurors admitted to knowing about the Carr case through the media. Each of the eighty-three prospective jurors, interviewed individually by Wagner and the prosecutor, said they could not be impartial. "They said right off the bat they felt I was guilty," Cottingham told Judge Galda.

However, Judge Galda's overriding concern with the Maryann Carr case going before a jury was not for the pretrial publicity about Cottingham. Galda agreed to hear the evidence himself because he felt that a jury might not be able to comprehend its responsibility to weigh evidence from other crimes. The bulk of the evidence and testimony would be a repeat from the 1981 trial, including the testimony of Miss O'Dell, who was savagely beaten on May 22, 1980, the day Cottingham was arrested. He reasoned that twelve laymen might have great difficulty listening to Leslie O'Dell tell them how she was kidnapped, placed in handcuffs, and raped, and then be expected to calmly determine that those events might only infer that Cottingham abducted and handcuffed Maryann Carr. A jurist, Galda suggested, is better equipped to dwell on these issues of modus operandi and identity. With a judge reviewing the evidence presented from prior convictions, there should be no question that the facts surrounding the murder of Valorie Street and the brutal attack on Miss O'Dell would not become the exclusive or primary foundation of evidence to convict Cottingham, at least not without other substantial evidence linking him to Maryann Carr.

"It's a very unusual step in any homicide trial," Judge Galda conceded on his decision to weigh the evidence himself. He also noted that he was a former prosecutor, having served in the Bergen County office in the mid-1960's. This last remark might have been construed as a warning that he, Judge Galda, would be tougher on Assistant Prosecutor Calo; but that was not to be the outcome.

# *Thirteen*

# Find an Old Signature

In terms of the timeframe of events surrounding the 1977 crime Richard Cottingham was charged with and the crimes he was convicted of committing after his first trial in 1981, there were two categories of witnesses. Among the 1977 witnesses, as they were to be called, were Jan Cousins, David E. Church, John Van Soest, Robert DeMartin, June Hamilton, and Catherine Ferrara. Of those six—and there were others of far less importance to the state's effort to tie Cottingham to Miss Carr—Van Soest and Church were the most important.

Jan Cousins, who lived across the hallway from the Carrs on the top floor of building 462 in Ledgewood Terrace, mainly contributed that there were voices coming from Miss Carr's apartment on the evening of December 15. She placed the time at about 7:30. Miss Cousins, who inferred that Michael and Maryann Carr had had loud arguments in the past, said she couldn't make out all the words, but one of the voices was Maryann's and she was arguing with another person. She testified that she understood only two words from Maryann: "I will . . . I will." The words were not uttered with a sound of defiance, the neighbor said. Miss Cousins described the voice as that of a terrified person. It was a scream, she said.

June Hamilton, the manager of Ledgewood Terrace, testified about the building and its tenants. She noted that she had been by Miss Carr's apartment on December 15, 1977, to drop off a security check. Robert DeMartin and Catherine Ferrara were important mainly from the standpoint of setting a timeframe for the events of the evening of the 15th. Catherine, Maryann's mother-in-law, was to have seen Maryann later that evening. But she grew worried and called the Carr apartment at about 7:50. It was a premonition, she testified, a feeling that something was wrong. She continued calling through the night with the same result, no response from Maryann. Catherine also called long distance to her son, Michael Carr, who was on a business trip to Rochester, New York. Finally, she called her nephew, Robert DeMartin, who lived a few buildings away from Maryann in building 468. Their conversation took place at about 10:50. DeMartin agreed to go to Maryann's apartment to check if anything was wrong. To Judge Galda, DeMartin's only significant contribution was confirmation that Maryann had been at home that night. One of her cigarettes was in an ashtray in the kitchen and a half-empty glass, apparently some kind of alcoholic beverage or cocktail, was left on the counter. The only thing the least out of place was a couch in the living room. The loveseat had been moved slightly, it appeared, but nothing was amiss, nothing turned over, nothing seemed missing. DeMartin, nevertheless, called Michael Carr and the husband agreed that the police should be notified.

Sometime between 7:30 and eight o'clock, David Church, a bachelor who lived in Maryann's building, was leaving for his night class at a school in Bergen County. Church testified that Maryann's red Camaro was parked two cars way from his own. He also testified that he saw Maryann Carr and a man he believed to be her husband. The two were standing near the Camaro, talking. Church got into his own car, put it in reverse, backed out, and, as he was starting forward, glanced in the rearview mirror. Again, he testified, he saw Maryann Carr with a man who looked like her husband. Michael Carr, who was about 350 miles from Little Ferry that night, stands about five feet ten inches and weighs some 170 pounds. In 1977, he was twenty-eight; he had light brown hair and a mustache. Judge Galda thought it was quite significant that David Church, not once but twice, testified that he thought the man with Maryann was Michael Carr. Richard Cottingham weighed about 187 pounds in 1977. He is five feet ten inches tall and he had a bushy mustache at that time.

Interestingly enough, there was more to David Church's statement when he was interviewed by the authorities in 1977, a few days after Maryann Carr disappeared and then was found dead at the Quality Inn parking area. This part of that statement did not come out in court: Church had told the police that Maryann and the mystery man he could not identify were hugging when he saw them in his rearview mirror; and Church also told police that the man with Maryann appeared a little taller than Michael Carr and somewhat thinner.

John Van Soest's testimony was about the all-important door key. He was Assistant Prosecutor Calo's most important 1977 witness because the key to the outside door of Building 462 was, according to Calo, the crucial link between Cottingham and Maryann. The key was among several items Van Soest said were missing after his apartment was robbed. But the state's witness and others who testified from his workplace, Blue Cross and Blue Shield in New York, also suggested that the key might have been misplaced or stolen at work, not during the robbery of Van Soest's apartment. Nevertheless, Van Soest testified that it was his key that was found in Richard Cottingham's safe the day authorities searched Cottingham's Lodi home.

Van Soest, Cottingham's friend and co-worker, also testified that the two men talked about the disappearance of Maryann Carr. Van Soest knew Miss Carr. One of his closest friends, a policeman who lived in Building 462, had been at Michael and Maryann's wedding in 1976. Van Soest socialized a great deal with others who lived in Building 462. Still, it was Richard Cottingham who thought it was odd the way Maryann was apparently abducted. One other important factor in the Van Soest-Cottingham "friendship" had to do with $15,000. Cottingham was going to loan Van Soest the money, but the two friends had a falling out over the terms of the loan. Judge Galda acknowledged there might be some "bias" in Van Soest's testimony, which included the following statement: "We couldn't understand how it could happen because to get in the building he'd have to have a special key." Van Soest's testimony related to some discussion he and Cottingham had about Maryann Carr a short time after her murder. "Cottingham told me if something like that happened [a person getting into her building with a "special key"], the girl would have to know somebody . . . or let him in voluntarily."

Van Soest's testimony also contributed some new significance to Robert DeMartin's earlier remarks about going to Maryann's apartment the night of December 15. DeMartin testified that he used his own key to open the outside door to Building 462. DeMartin lived in Building 468. Judge Galda noted this oddity, but he blithely moved on to other matters. DeMartin had said he had never before used the key to get into Building 462. "It was just happenstance, why that key seemed to fit," Judge Galda remarked. Court observers were left to wonder how many of the other building keys fit Building 462.

The second category of witnesses, including Leslie Ann O'Dell, were those the state called to testify about Cottingham's other crimes. While he originally had intended to bring out every piece of evidence from the Susan Geiger and Karen Schilt abductions, the prosecutor limited the evidence to the Valorie Street murder and Miss O'Dell's experience. These witnesses also included all the investigators, the forensic experts, the employees of the Quality Inn, and the Federal Bureau of Investigation's expert on fingerprint analysis. Most important among this group, it turned out, were the medical authorities who had examined Valorie Street and Maryann Carr. In all, Judge Galda had fifty-seven witnesses testify in the ten days of trial and he admitted 185 pieces of evidence, the majority of which were from the Street and O'Dell convictions.

But it was the doctors who convicted Richard Cottingham of Maryann Carr's murder. They did it with the interpretations they made of the five-year-old autopsy on Maryann Carr. And, perhaps more important, Dr. Louis V. Napolitano provided Judge Galda with the deciding evidence. Napolitano, whose testimony caused a minor stir when it was revealed that one of his associates had known Maryann Carr in more than a professional sense, presented a survey of murders committed in Bergen County over a ten-year period. With Dr. John Aprovian's interpretation of his own examination of Maryann Carr's body and his own autopsy of Valorie Street, Dr. Napolitano came to some very concrete conclusions.

"I thought I was looking at the same case," he testified. Napolitano had studied 200 murder cases. Ten of the cases were murder by strangulation. And when he reviewed the autopsies of Street and Carr, the doctor told Judge Galda, they were identical.

Maryann Carr was wearing two pieces of jewelry when she was murdered, a ring her husband had given her on their first anniversary and a gold chain necklace. The fact that they were still on her body and not stolen was significant enough, but Dr. Aprovian found more significance in the necklace.

On December 17, 1977, when the first press reports were published about Maryann Carr, Dr. Aprovian was quoted as saying his initial finding was death by strangulation. The gold chain, he theorized, had been used as a ligature to choke Maryann to death.

This theory, then-Prosecutor Roger W. Breslin, Jr., announced the following day at a news conference, was incorrect. Dr. Aprovian, the prosecutor told new reporters on December 18, 1977, had changed his mind after the more extensive autopsy was performed on December 17, the day after Maryann's body was found. The assistant medical examiner had found that Maryann's lungs had collapsed, Breslin said, and his final conclusion was that the twenty-six-year-old woman had died of suffocation. This could have meant she was either choked or even smothered. Interestingly enough, the detective assigned to attend the December 17 autopsy listened as Dr. Aprovian discovered the collapsed lungs. John Scioli, an investigator with the county prosecutor's office, recorded in his notes on the autopsy that Dr. Aprovian determined Maryann's death was caused by "asphyxia due to suffocation." When Scioli was called to testify in the October, 1982, trial, he announced that he had lost or misplaced his notes on Dr. Aprovian's remarks. But when he testified, and Dr. Napolitano testified about his survey and the comparison made between the Street and Carr cause of death, the interpretation was back to strangulation by a ligature. There was a scratch on Maryann's neck that determined she had been choked with a ligature. How it could have been done with her flimsy, gold chain necklace, however, is anyone's guess.

Midway through the trial, which began September 28 with opening statements, Cottingham apeared to be becoming more agitated. He had heard all the same employees of the Quality Inn testify to the day when Valorie Street's body was found in room 132, and he listened to the detail-by-detail rehash of the events of May 22, 1980, when Leslie Ann O'Dell screamed for help, bringing police to room 117 of the same motel. Cottingham sat through Patrolman Stanley Melowic's version of that day when he shouted to Cottingham to halt, frisked him, and made the biggest arrest of his career. But it was on Monday, October 4, that the reality of where this trial was going began to sink into the curly-blond-haired defendant's head.

It was during that Monday's session that Dr. Napolitano presented his survey and remarked about the uniquely similar methods used to strangle Valorie Street and Maryann Carr. Cottingham could hear Assistant Prosecutor Dennis Calo's words come crushing down again, like a shrill echoe in stereophonic sound. *The distinctive style used to murder these two women was the defendant's signature!* It amounted to Richard Cottingham's "carving his name into the bodies of Maryann Carr and Valorie Ann Street." Calo put strong emphasis on Dr. Napolitano's conclusion, shouting his indicting words again, Cottingham must have thought. "I thought I was looking at the same case," Dr. Napolitano had declared, in reference to the ligature strangulation, the marks on the ankles from the handcuffs, and the marks from the tape on the mouth. It could have been at this particularly damning stage of the prosecutor's case when Cottingham thought to himself, I've got to get out of here. I have to run.

It all happened during the afternoon break. Two sheriff's deputies were bringing Cottingham out of the men's room, just across the hallway from Judge Galda's chambers on the third floor of the courthouse. Normally the defendant would be in leg irons and handcuffs. But Judge Galda, a thoughtful man known for his compassion, insisted that Cottingham not be chained coming in and out of his courtroom. Waiting for just the right moment, the strapping, five foot ten inch prisoner flung his navy blue sports jacket at the guards and bolted down the hallway to an exit. The two guards, momentarily startled, ran after him, but Cottingham had a good head start. He sped down three flights of stairs, jogged past the main door to the jail, and ran across a parking lot to the corner of Church and Court streets in downtown Hackensack. Breathing heavily, he looked away from the courthouse for a few seconds, uncertain which way was best. It turned out to be a second too long. A posse of ten sheriff's deputies came rushing across the street, quicker than double time. One guard tackled the defendant, bringing him crashing to the sidewalk, while two others reached out with shackles. Five minutes of freedom on a balmy fall day. The fresh air was still in his lungs as the guard led him back to the third-floor holding pen. For a man faced with nearly 200 years in maximum security, those several moments outside must have felt like a week of Sundays.

Judge Galda, who could share much of the fault for the lack of security, remarked that the incident was more an embarrassment than anything more serious. The prosecutor, of course, attributed Cottingham's burst for freedom to the state's building case for a guilty verdict. Frank Wagner told the judge that his client bolted because of sheer boredom and disgust over the prosecutor's repetitious evidence. Ultimately, Judge Galda said he would draw no strong inference from the attempted escape. But one wonders if that is really what the judge was thinking. When he announced just after the incident that the trial would continue without interruption, Judge Galda remarked, "another question is whether this may be construed as an indication of guilt when he tries to flee."

"Now, needless to say, that this has been quite a responsibility and burden when one considers the many days of trial." Judge Fred C. Galda spoke of the "unusual procedure" he had hoisted upon himself as he began to explain the reasons for his conclusion on the charge of murder. It was October 12, a Tuesday. The judge had taken the long Columbus Day weekend to study and review the evidence and testimony, and then announced that he was ready to render his verdict. He painstakingly recited each and every major portion of testimony in chronological order, leaving what he considered the most important, Dr. Louis Napolitano's, for last.

Cottingham almost seemed prepared for the worst. It was his lawyer who during the final arguemnts had burst into tears, who stared uneasily at the judge, while the defendant coldly eyed Galda through his wire-rimmed glasses. It was as if he could read ahead to the judge's final thoughts.

"So there seems to be no question," Judge Galda's voice raised a bit, coming near the end of more than an hour of reviewing almost each person's testimony. "No question, and the court finds as a fact that in respect to the Street and the Carr cases, they are similar in that adhesive tape and handcuffs were used in both instances.

And, they both were strangled." Judge Galda made some surprising excusatory comments about Dr. Napolitano's "scientific" survey. It might have been helpful, he said, if the survey had been broader in scope, had perhaps included the surrounding counties. The judge also noted the discrepancy in the way Street and Carr were strangled. (Judge Huot had placed greater emphasis on this same observation. On Street, the ligature was tightened to the right, while on Carr, the ligature was pulled to the left.) Judge Galda had this explanation: "Of course, Dr. Napolitano said, in respect to the ligature which is on one side, it would only come about depending on the position that you were standing in, whether it was from the right or from the left."

Frank Wagner's thoughts went back to Judge Huot's other comments about the dissimilarities. But he could only hope that this judge would have taken the same trouble to consider not only similarities and dissimilarities, but what also might be coincidences. Like two bodies ending up at the same motel. But that fleeting moment of hope vanished with Judge Galda's next heavy pronouncement.

"So, while the burden of proof in that regard is on the prosecution as well as where they have to find convincing proof, I find not only is the testimony in regard to the similarity referred to clear and convincing, but it satisfies this court even to the extent as to the prior occasions that the modus operandi in respect to these cases are so unique and so novel as to be personal to himself. And, I find that to be so beyond a reasonable doubt, that it had to be the handiwork of Richard Cottingham in this case. I find that to be a fact."

Cottingham was by himself at the defense table. He sat with his head bowed in his hands, his elbows apart. Off in another part of the courtroom, Michael Carr stood nearby his dead wife's father, Anthony Gangemi. "Justice was done," Maryann's father muttered.

# Epilogue

Item: NEW YORK (UPI)—The bound, nude body of a woman whose throat had been slashed was found Wednesday in the Ramada Inn in Manhattan, police said.

The body of the unidentified woman was discovered at 3 p.m. in room 624 of the hotel at 796 Eighth Avenue.

The woman's hands and feet were bound together with tape, police said, and her throat had been slashed.

That item came over the United Press wire service on October 6, 1982, just a week before Richard Cottingham was found guilty of the strangulation murder of Maryann Carr. The day after Judge Fred C. Galda announced his decision, Robert M. Morgenthau, the Manhattan District attorney, announced that his office would start the procedure to transfer Richard Cottingham to New York's jurisdiction for the trial on three murder indictments, including the celebrated Times Square torso murders.

Paul Beakmon grimaced when he saw the headline screaming across the top of the page: NUDE TORTURED, SLAIN IN

MIDTOWN HOTEL. He laid down his copy of the New York *Post* and took a long swallow from his beer. Nearly three years and a few additional grey hairs measured the time since he had last seen a prostitute subjected to such torture. He sucked the last foamy gulp from the bottle and angrily threw it in the trash. He thought of Richard Cottingham and reminded himself to call his contact over in New Jersey and find out how that trial for the nurse's murder was moving along.

Who the hell is this guy? Beakmon asked himself. Sure as hell it wasn't Cottingham who brutalized the hooker at the Ramada Inn. Besides, there was a new wrinkle to this one. This prostitute, whose hands, feet, and mouth were bound with electrician's tape before her jugular vein was severed with one powerful slash, was black. The ones in 1979 and 1980, the murders at the Travel Inn and the Hotel Seville, were all white hookers. Beakmon knew that even if Cottingham were loose, he couldn't be blamed for this one. Cottingham's targets were always white women, preferably blonde and reasonably attractive.

Still, Beakmon, always willing to play devil's advocate, couldn't dismiss the one strong similarity: The young victim, probably about twenty-five years old, had been tortured for hours. She obviously knew her attacker, having signed into the hotel room. She was left on the floor of room 624, her body nude. The telltale signs of her torture included severe burn marks on the palms of each hand. Dozens of spent matches were strewn around the room. Sergeant Beakmon, who would be called to testify in Cottingham's pending trials for three prostitute murders in 1979 and 1980, recalled with painful ease that the hotel rooms where Jean Reyner, Deedah Goodarzi, and the third, unidentified hooker were butchered were also set on fire. He wondered if this latest prostitute murder might be a belated copycat who just didn't have time to strike a last match before he finished his grisly deed.

But Sergeant Beakmon knew enough not to make waves. He knew the brass downtown wanted those three homicides closed out. The Manhattan District Attorney's office had tried its best to get

Cottingham to plea. Beakmon grinned and shook his head at the guy's stubborn refusal to admit to the killings. Imagine somebody already faced with nearly 200 years behind bars still insisting he's innocent, insisting on another trial, Beakmon thought to himself. Anyway, this recent thing at the Ramada Inn had to be the work of some wacky bastard who finally got up the nerve to get himself a prostitute. The guy probably wasn't even around New York in '79 and '80. Beakmon tried his best to drive the thought from his mind. He had twenty years under his belt. Retirement was right around the corner. Retirement and a chance to buy that boat he'd always wanted and haul it on down to some quiet, desolate place off the coast of the Carolinas. Maybe then he could even get the opportunity for a reunion with Karen. She was a little older now, much more mature. It would be nice, he thought, if his daughter could join him for a vacation trip. It would be a good start for his retirement and a new life.

Paul Beakmon thought about his future and he reflected on all the things in life a man of forty-eight might consider. He was a cop, but more important, he was an honest cop. That was no small claim for a veteran of nearly twenty years on the New York Police Department. He was a father and, as much as that often served to remind him of his failed marriage, he loved his daughter, even on an absentee basis. But when he looked in the mirror after each morning's shave, Beakmon, a descendant of proud Dutch shippers, saw the worn face of a stubborn cop. He never could just drift with the tide and he never would. He decided he'd avoid official lines of communication, but would look at the October 6, 1982, prostitute murder in the Ramada Inn. He just couldn't dismiss the similarities to the three slayings he'd investigated back in 1980, and, just as he remained certain that Deedah Goodarzi, Jean Reyner, and Ms. X were all the demonic victims of one man, Richard Cottingham, the policeman was also sure he could never rest comfortably until he had personally satisfied himself that the Ramada Inn slashing was the isolated, nevertheless brutal act of a maniacal copycat. And even if his mind might rest from the thought, Paul Beakmon knew that the ever-active pit of his stomach would not permit him to forget his duties as a cop.

The Street-Carr murders and prostitute kidnappings provided elements that easily made the cases among the most sensational in Bergen County's history, and possibly the New York metropolitan area when one includes the carnage Richard Cottingham was credited with conducting in nearby Manhattan. Certainly in the decades since World War II, no murderer had been captured in Bergen County who could come close to matching Cottingham's sheer contept for human life.

This is not to suggest that this section of the country did not produce other criminal episodes to contribute to the nation's fascination with bizarre behavior. After all, this was the county that gave us Edgar Smith, who ravaged the body of fifteen-year-old high school cheerleader Victoria Zielinski, leaving her remains in a quarry in Ramsey, New Jersey. Smith, twenty-three at the time he was prosecuted for the 1957 murder, finally got around to admitting the crime more than twenty years later, much to the discomfort of his staunch defender, conservative columnist-author William F. Buckely, Jr. And it was in Bergen County one warm August morning in 1963 that a Brooklyn man ordered two Lodi cops, one just twenty-one and not even officially sworn to duty, to strip to their shorts and entertain a handful of early morning revelers at the Angel Lounge bar. When the entertainment was finished, a police sergeant and his rookie-partner lay side-by-side in a pool of blood. One of the assassins was killed within days by a team of New York City police, directed to find Frank Falco in a seedy Manhattan hotel. The other, a somewhat noted painter, author, and counselor of teenaged law breakers, still claims he was too drunk to know what was happening while his partner filled the two cops with holes. Thomas "Tommie the Rabbi" Trantino may never get out, and he'll probably live longer because of it.

But the Cottingham case did more than catch the attention of every woman and every woman's husband, boyfriend, and father.

"This is the man, the master," the young prosecutor bellowed. "He, himself, says on the stand, 'I enjoy this. I enjoy seeing women cringe in fear of me.'" Dennis Calo continued his attack: "We deal here with women who had their most intimate privacy violated, who were littered like so much garbage by Richard Cottingham." This man was operating in a time when the sins of illegal abortionists were being brought up by feminists in ardent challenge to the Right-to-Life conservative view that women did not have the choice over the fate of their bodies. And it was in this era that millions of women and their loved ones were becoming increasingly convinced of the merits of the need for the ultimately ill-fated Equal Rights Amendment. Cottingham's callous abuses were those of an extreme enemy of the female's fight for liberation.

Here was a husband, the father of three small children, who, in the course of cheating on his faithful wife, purportedly went through his nights in search of nurses who were an easy mark and punishing other women who sold their bodies. Those with thinking minds, able to journey beyond the lurid details of women shackled in handcuffs and subjected to the most brutal sexual atrocities, found it profoundly disturbing that such a Neanderthal attitude toward women found itself acted out by a single individual. But of far more troubling concern was the claim that Cottingham was an unofficial member of a growing sex cult. Dr. Park Elliot Dietz, the prominent Harvard University psychiatrist who helped confirm the suspicions of a great many Americans when he deduced that would-be presidential assassin John W. Hinckley, Jr., was out of his mind, suggested that Cottingham was one of thousands of people on the borderline or deeply involved in a wide variety of perversions, bondage, and sado-masochism.

But Assistant Prosecutor Dennis Calo, the man primarily responsible for insuring that Richard Cottingham would not see the prison gate over his shoulder in this lifetime, did not indulge in any intellectural diatribe in his sustained, often melodramatic assault on Cottingham's stubborn denials. Nor, surprisingly, did this young, ambitious lawyer seem to seek more than his due credit for the performance. In fact, Calo was exceedingly modest, even shy, about his achievement. Calo did not easily warm up to the idea that he should speak to the press. One newspaper reporter found it amusing how the prosecutor often had the words, "No comment," on his lips before a question was even asked. Once when the question merely pertained to establishing a key date on one of the Cottingham court hearings, Calo insisted on speaking off the record. This kind of conduct, attributed to inexperience and a personality trait described by some as brash, slowly disappeared as he became more confident of the outcome.

Dennis Calo's style in the courtroom could be described in a word: zealous. He toned down his sharp, often loud, verbal jabs as the first trial wore on, but it is not surprising that he might be accused of an almost vicious approach to his role. His performance was in stark contrast to the low-key, almost understated appearance displayed by his adversary, the seasoned defense attorney Donald R. Conway. But if Calo can be faulted for unnecessary courtroom theatrics, Conway could have made more effort to conceal his disinterested, seemingly strained attention to his client's needs. None of this, of course, was lost on the defendant's sister, Carol Jacobsen.

Carol grew to despise both Dennis Calo and her brother's lawyer. She indicted Calo for the lies and distortions that were woven together to form the web of false charges against Richard. And she accused Conway with taking on the defense at a high retainer and then deserting Richard at his most difficult hour.

"How can anyone say that a man who has been front-page news for the last year and a half can be given a fair trial in Bergen County?" Carol demanded, lashing out at Calo in an interview with *The Record* of Hackensack. Calo, who was the thirty-three-year-old chief of the Bergen County homicide squad when the Cottingham investigation got underway in May of 1980, insisted from the start that Cottingham should and would receive a fair and impartial hearing of the charges. The assistant prosecutor relented not an inch in his demand for a jury trial, arguing that the community and the family of the victims deserved to have the highly provocative indictment heard by a jury of the defendant's peers. His insistence that a jury trial was necessary came under the most adverse conditions for impartiality, however. Long before the first trial, the media documented some of the most obscure details of the crimes, including the existence of Cottingham's "Trophy Room" found to contain the most incriminating evidence of the victims' jewelry and clothing. One psychiatrist, Dr. James A. Brussel of New York City's "Mad Bomber" fame, suggested the taking of the victims' personal items had a fetishistic element to it. Dr. Brussel, who also examined Albert De Salvo, the Boston Strangler, speculated that this might mean Cottingham wanted to take possession of his victims. The press coverage of the case, one that brought together all the elements of good reading, was warranted, even if it may have gone too far—for example, the presence in the courtroom of network television cameras the day Cottingham was sentenced. Unfortunately, the press also deserted Cottingham by failing to look over the court system's shoulder at crucial stages of the state's inventiveness, choosing instead the general sensation.

Carol Jacobsen, unrelenting in her belief that some conspiracy was behind her brother's troubles, thought she could answer the question she posed not long before Bergen County was prepared to go into court on the second murder trial. "It's all a game being played by the prosecution," she charged. "We, the people, are the fools if we let this happen." The gutsy Florida housewife accused the prosecutor by name, saying Dennis Calo was "using his personal vendetta against Richard to further his career."

Calo, a slight man with a strikingly boyish face, set off by a head of closely cropped dark hair, was, by the conclusion of Cottingham's first trial, two years older and more seasoned. His office was immersed in the investigation into a young woman's senseless death from the metal fragments of a homemade bomb, apparently meant for her boyfriend. "Well, Dennis," a courthouse visitor spoke as the lawyer backed away from a urinal in the men's lavatory on the second level of the aging county building. He paused to dry his hands as the visitor continued his sentence. "How is that big case of yours coming along?" (referring to the Maryann Carr murder). Calo hesitated, glancing in the mirror to straighten his tie. "Which case is that," he asked, typical of his air of nonchalance. "Oh," he acknowledged, "it's just like every other one. Moving ahead." It was only a matter of weeks, at that point, before Calo would win the second most significant conviction of his short, but increasingly bright law enforcement career. "There is no personal vendetta," Calo told a reporter on another occasion. The Maryann Carr murder, he said, "is just another case that has to be tried."

At the close of 1982, the Bergen County Prosecutor's office was striving to close another highly sensational murder case, that of Debi Bell, the nightclub singer. There were indictments to be sought on some gambling violations and on a number of government corruption allegations. The office was also coping with some political uncertainties. An acting prosecutor had been dispatched from the state attorney general's office in the state capital at Trenton. The state was trying to keep the county's highest law enforcement office in operation while a powerfully influential state senator continued to block the governor's choice of a new prosecutor, a Republican, to replace Roger W. Breslin, Jr., a Democrat who resigned that year to return to private practice. The office's top assistant prosecutor, Robert Leaman, had also resigned. Dennis Calo was one of a handful of the office's twenty-five assistants who was in line for the first assistant's job.

If she, her elderly mother, and her imprisoned brother could find no justice in the trials Richard received in Bergen County, perhaps Carol Jacobsen saw poetic justice in the fate of the lawyer Carol accused of standing by the side of the tracks while the system railroaded her brother. She had the most sinister ideas of who and what did Richard in, but even Carol, as much as she grew to deeply resent Donald R. Conway, never dreamed that he himself was in the middle of a serious criminal scheme that would explode like a bomb, sending fragments across New Jersey, resulting in direct hits on the reputations and careers of two of the state's most prominent attorneys and uncovering an unholy alliance between one of the country's major mob leaders and the man who was once president of the New Jersey Bar Association.

It all began on July 19, 1981, about midway between Cottingham's conviction and his sentencing for the prostitute tortures. Peter Doyne, Conway's junior assistant, had assumed primary responsibility for cleaning up the final odds and ends of the Cottingham matter before the sentencing, set for July 25. Conway's career had long reached salient heights with such clients as former Secretary of State J. Edward Crabiel and Stephen Andretta, a New Jersey-Genovese-mob lieutenant whose brother, Thomas was one of those in the Tony Provenzano gang suspected in the kidnapping-assassination of Jimmy Hoffa. It was later apparent why Doyne's senior associate had more important matters on his mind.

In the wee hours of that July 19, Phillip Lombardo, Jr., the pugnacious stepson of Phillip "Cockeyed Phil" Lombardo of Englewood, New Jersey, was being booted out the front door of a rock nightclub on the Jersey Shore. It was about the third time Philly Jr. had been bounced that night, but this time he decided to retaliate by spraying a little chemical mace on the bouncer, who just happened to be a cop employed by the New Jersey State Police. Things got out of hand and the upshot of the incident had the trooper, Denis McDowell, charging Philly with assault. Now Philly, who drunkenly boasted to anyone who would listen that he and his relatives were bigtime in the New York rackets, realized when he sobered up that he was in serious soup; he had to have some fancy legal advice on how to get around this beef with McDowell. His father, "Cockeyed Phil," part of the Who's Who in the family of Vito Genovese and Frank Tieri, knew who to contact in the legal community. He hired Donald Conway to defend the boy, who, after all, was just a hothead kid in a sticky jam. It was a jam, however, that wouldn't look good on junior's record, and it was the wise guys in Lombardo's New Jersey family who wanted to do what they could to stave off any possible embarrassment to the old man.

Among "Cockeyed Phil's" minions was a local wise guy from Cottingham's former town. Alan "Little Al" Grecco, who lived across town from Cottingham's house in Lodi, and a few of his pals came up with the idea to pay the state cop ten grand to change a few things in the arrest report he'd made out on the night of July 19. All the cop had to do was downgrade the complaint to creating a disturbance, or disorderly conduct, or, maybe, just drop the whole thing as a misunderstanding. With Conway hired as Philly's lawyer and the wise guys putting together a bribe offer, the effort to get this kid off on something like being kicked out of a nightclub seemed pretty ridiculous. But one man who was watching over the scheme said the whole matter may have been dismissed as a silly maneuver by some small-time mobsters had it not been elevated to the level of involving one of the state's eminent trial attorneys, Don Conway, who was once considered for a state judgeship. As it turned out, McDowell refused to go along and instead reported the offer to his superiors. Another state cop who was playing go-between for the wise guys agreed to wear a body mike for a few crucial meetings with Grecco, Conway, and a couple of others, including Vincent Rigolosi, president of the Bergen County Bar Association.

Conway, testifying at his own trial on charges of witness tampering and conspiracy, protested his innocence and denied even knowing who "Cockeyed Phil" Lombardo was. The jury found that incredible, especially after listening to a tape of one recorded meeting in which the undercover cop asked Conway if Genovese crime family boss Philip Lombardo, Sr., had been shown a copy of Trooper McDowell's arrest report. The attorney replied: "I mean, you hit the nail right on the head." In the judge's view, Conway went out to hit a home run for his client, the mob boss. He just tried too hard, the wrong way.

On November 4, 1982, just about a month after Cottingham was convicted for the murder of Maryann Carr, his former attorney was in another courtroom, about forty-five miles south of Hackensack in a place called Tom's River, N.J. He stood at the defense table, but this time it was as the defendant.

"I was watching Conway," a juror who helped convict the lawyer later told a reporter for *The Record* of Hackensack. "When the first 'guilty' came out, I saw his head drop." Conway was found guilty for conspiracy and witness tampering. His attorney launched a vigorous appeal, demanding a new trial because one of the witnesses against Conway allegedly lied. But Superior Court Judge William H. Huber rejected Conway's requests. He sentenced Conway to four years and fined him $2,500. The four-year prison term was suspended, however; Conway continued on probation. His real punishment, unless appeals of Judge Huber's decision are upheld, is yet to be decided. The former state Bar Association president will be permitted to continue his practice of law until the state's highest court hears an ethics complaint and decides if Conway should be suspended or disbarred.

Besides the hardship and pain, there were several bitter ironies sprinkled throughout the nightmare that Janet Cottingham endured because of her husband's sexual proclivities and the punishment his actions brought on him and his family. It was a horrible awakening for Janet, even though she had long suspected her husband's infedelity. Learning that he had brutally tortured and murdered a teenaged prostitute on May 3, 1980, the day after their tenth wedding anniversary was, perhaps, the first real shock to her otherwise naïve outlook on life and her marriage. But as much as what he had done left her with feelings of resentment and contempt for Richard, Janet demonstrated extraordinary strength. The divorce suit she had filed in 1979 provided evidence of the scars of years of uncertainty, shame, and neglect. Now, when she could readily be forgiven for abandoning him, Janet refused. She withdrew the divorce, deciding she would think it over. That was in June, 1980. No longer able to stand the whispers and rumors surrounding her husband, however, Janet did decide to move away from their little Cape Cod home in Lodi. She and the children moved to Poughkeepsie, New York, about thirty miles north of Hackensack, where she rented an apartment and got herself a part-time job.

It was obvious from her testimony in the 1981 trial that Janet was as nervous and uncomfortable answering the prosecutor's questions as she was stubbornly defensive. Through it all, she still supported Richard. After all, he was the father of her three children, who were far too young to understand the full impact of the charges and the trials. All three were attending school by 1982. Jenny, the youngest, had started first grade, and Scott, their son, was seven, just a grade ahead of Jenny. The oldest son, it appeared, might have the most difficult time sorting all this out some day. No father to help him with his school work; no father to hold him and assure him everything would be okay the first time he was left with a broken heart; no real father there for birthdays.

October 15, 1982, was another birthday come and gone for Blair. There would be little sense in telling Jenny, who would be six that October 13, that her father would not be returning home until she has grown and had her own children. And Blair, his oldest son and probably his favorite child, could not be expected to understand the significance of Judge Fred C. Galda's statement on October 15, 1982, the boy's ninth birthday, when the judge looked at Richard Cottingham and asked: "What mitigating factors could there possibly be to such an offense as testfied to and shown in this case?" For the murder of Maryann Carr, Judge Galda gave Cottingham twenty-five years to life, placing a mandatory minimum of thirty years in prison. The term was to be served consecutively with the previous murder conviction sentence.

Adding together the terms for each murder conviction and the multiple convictions for rape, assault, and kidnapping, Cottingham would serve more than 200 years for the New Jersey crimes. But several of the terms were made concurrent, meaning Cottingham's actual computed time behind bars would be more like 125 years, with eligibility for parole in approximately forty-seven years. He was thirty-six when he was sentenced. "The bottom line is he'll probably never see the light of day," a grim-faced Dennis Calo remarked.

On March 30, 1983, a state judge in Trenton, N.J., listened intently as a New York City detective disclosed crucial elements of the evidence that would be used to prosecute Cottingham for the infamous 1979 torso murders.

Contained in the detective's testimony, needed by the judge for his decision on a request to transfer the defendant to Manhattan for trial in a New York State Supreme Court, were some of the facts about the New York investigation. As Detective Michael Clark told it, Richard Cottingham carefully planned the maniacal bloodbath for the two headless victims found in a burned-out room at a Times Square motel on December 2, 1979. And the detective's testimony officially confirmed what had long been public speculation. The murderer took pieces of the victims' jewelry, placed them in his safe, and saved them for reasons only Richard Cottingham could reveal.

A few of the details about the murders had never been revealed. First there was the telephone call to the Travel Inn Motor Lodge. Detective Clark said that someone in the computer control room at Cottingham's place of employment—Blue Cross and Blue Shield of Greater New York—telephoned the Travel Inn at 515 West 42nd Street on November 26, 1979. The male caller reserved a room for November 29 through December 2. Dozens of Blue Cross employees were interviewed about the call, but only one was suspected of making it. Cottingham had worked the four-to-midnight shift November 26.

Next there was the signature of the fictitious Carl Wilson of Anderson Place, Merlin, New Jersey.

Detective Clark said the defendant signed the hotel registration card on November 29 and was given Room 417. He was rarely seen during the four-day period he reserved the room. "Carl Wilson's" signature was compared with the writing of the man suspected of making the room reservation, Detective Clark said, and an expert determined the writings were made by Richard Cottingham.

But it was not until the third week of May, 1980, that New York City investigators homed in on their prime suspect.

Richard Cottingham had been arrested May 22 leaving a Hasbrouck Heights, N.J., motel, with Leslie Ann O'Dell inside, badly beaten. Detectives soon appeared at his Lodi, N.J., home with court-approved search warrants. Investigators searched the entire house, but they ultimately concentrated on a basement room that contained a small, office-sized safe. A ring and a necklace in the safe demanded the attention of the New York detectives. Detective Clark said the jewelry was shown to two acquaintances of Deedah Goodarzi, the one torso murder victim authorities were able to identify. Both of Deedah's friends asserted that the ring and the necklace belonged to the brutally slain twenty-two-year-old prostitute.

Judge A. Jerome Moore weighed Detective Clark's testimony against arguments made by Cottingham's court-appointed attorney. The defendant, looking drawn and pale in his drab prison-issue shirt and jeans, stared pensively at the judge. Judge Moore concluded that the testimony "more than supports the reasonable assumption" that Cottingham was in New York at the locations asserted to by Detective Clark. The judge ordered the defendant to be transferred to Manhattan for trial.

# For the Record

Richard Francis Cottingham; 29 Vreeland Street, Lodi, New Jersey; DOB 25 November 1946; white male, 5-feet-10, approximately 175-180 pounds, light brown hair, blue eyes; occupation, computer operator.

*Record of criminal charges and convictions*:

DATE: JURISDICTION: CHARGE/CONVICTION: DISPOSITION

Oct. 3, 1969: New York City: intoxicated driving: 10 days jail, $50 fine.

Aug. 21, 1972: Paramus: shoplifting Stern's Dept. Store: $50 fine (8/30/72).

Sept. 4, 1973: New York City: robbery, sodomy, sexual assault: dismissed.

Feb. 12, 1974: New York City: unlawful imprisonment, robbery: dismissed.

May 22, 1980: Hasbrouck Heights: attempted murder of Leslie Ann O'Dell: *see below* for disposition of indictment.

Aug. 14, 1980: New York City: triple homicide—Mary Ann Jean Reyner; May 15, 1980; Deedeh Goodarzi and "Jane Doe," Nov. 29-Dec. 2, 1979: pending trial.

Sept. 17, 1980: Bergen County: 21-count indictment: *see below*:

KAREN SCHILT, Mar. 22-23, 1978: kidnapping, atrocious assault, robbery; SUSAN GEIGER, Oct. 12-13, 1978: kidnapping, rape, sodomy, robbery, atrocious assault; PAMELA WEISENFELD, May 12, 1980: kidnapping; VALORIE STREET, May 4, 1980: murder; LESLIE ANN O'DELL, May 22, 1980: kidnapping, attempted murder, aggravated assault, aggravated assault with deadly weapon, aggravated sexual assault while armed (rape), aggravated sexual assault while armed (sodomy), aggravated sexual assault while armed (fellatio), possession of a weapon; also possession of controlled dangerous substance, Secobarbital and Amobarbital, or Tulenol, and possession of controlled dangerous substance, Diazepam or Valium.

June 11, 1981: Bergen County: convicted on 15 of 20 counts: sentence July 25, 1981 to 173-197 years in state prison. Not guilty of robbery of Schilt, not guilty on Pamela Weisenfeld kidnapping, not guilty on anal sodomy of Geiger, rape of Geiger thrown out by judge for lack of evidence, not guilty on attempted murder of Leslie O'Dell, not guilty on aggravated assault of O'Dell. Sentence calculated after applying concurrent terms for multiple kidnap and assault convictions. Cottingham's prison term for the 1981 sentence is 60-95 years.

*One homicide charge in the 21-count indictment was severed. The Dec. 15, 1977, murder of Maryann Carr tried separately.

Oct. 1982: Bergen County: nonjury trial resulted in conviction for second degree murder of Maryann Carr, October 15, 1982, sentence 25 years to life, with a minimum term of 30 years to be served consecutively with the 1980 murder sentence.

On March 30, 1983, New Jersey Superior Court Judge Jerome Moore ordered Cottingham removed from the maximum security state prison in Trenton and transferred to the men's house of detention, Borough of Manhattan, New York State, for trial on the August, 1980 charges of murdering Deedeh Goodarzi, "Jane Doe," and Jean Reyner.